I0144964

THE LAW OF PRAYER:

God Does *Nothing*

But in

Answer to Prayer

THE LAW OF PRAYER:

God Does *Nothing*

But in

Answer to Prayer

B. J. WILLHITE

Hisway
Prayer Publications
P.O. Box 762
Jamul, CA 91935

The Law of Prayer:
God Does Nothing but in Answer to Prayer
ISBN 978-1-879545-17-5
Copyright © 2021 by B.J. Willhite
All rights reserved
Printed in the United States of America

Published by Hisway Prayer Publications
P.O. BOX 762
Jamul, CA 91935

This book was originally published as *Looking for a Better Way to Pray*, ISBN 978-1-4500-4230-7
Copyright © 2010 by B.J. Willhite
All rights reserved

No part of this book may be reproduced in any form including electronic, mechanical, photocopying without permission in writing from the publisher Hisway Prayer Publications.
Unless otherwise indicated, all Scripture quotations are taken from the New International Version, of the Bible, Copyright © 1978 by New York International Bible Society. Used by permission. All quotations from the Amplified Bible, Expanded Edition are marked AMP: The Zondervan Corporation and Lockman Foundation 1987. Used by permission. All quotations from the New King James Version Bible are marked NKJV. Thomas Nelson 1982. Used by permission. All quotations from The Living Bible Paraphrased Reference Edition are marked TLB. Tyndale House Publishers 1980.Used by permission.

Authors Comment:

In one of his books, E.M. Bounds attributed the following quote to John Wesley: *"God does nothing but in answer to prayer."* I read this as a young preacher and for some reason believed it. This conviction has been the strength of my ministry for more than 60 years. Though I would not say God does *absolutely nothing* but in answer to prayer, I will say, as a rule, God does nothing but in answer to believing prayer. – B. J. Willhite

> **Give me one hundred preachers who fear nothing but sin and desire nothing but God, and I care not a straw whether they be clergymen or laymen; such alone will shake the gates of hell and set up the kingdom of heaven on earth.* **God does nothing but in answer to prayer.**
>
> **-- John Wesley**

*Power Through Prayer, E.M. Bounds, Chapter 17, Preface, Baker House

Dedication

To Velma, my wife and prayer partner
For over 50 years

Contents

Preface

It was the spring of 1988. I had just decided to move to Washington, D.C. to establish the National Prayer Embassy when I sat down to write my first book, *Why Pray?* For several years, I was encouraged and challenged to write a book on the subject of prayer. However, I hesitated to do so because I had mixed feelings about it. I doubted myself and my ability to do the job. I was not sure I knew enough about prayer to positively contribute to the number of books already on the market about that subject. Nevertheless, due to the insistence of friends I contacted at Creation House, now known as Charisma House, I started to write.

It was May. The days were warm and the birds were singing as I sat down under a large pecan tree in Dallas to write. I determined to pen ten pages each day until the book was finished. So, with my legal pad in hand and some sharp pencils, I plunged into my mission. I always felt writing a book would be very difficult. Hence, I dreaded the thought of even starting. But as I sat and put pen to paper, I could not write as fast as the words were coming to me. The very anointing I often felt as I stood in the pulpit to proclaim the unsearchable riches of God's grace and truth came upon me.

Why Pray? was released a few months later and to my amazement, it began to sell. I had always thought a few friends and perhaps some of my relatives might want a copy but did not dream it would be printed six times by the publisher and in several other languages including German, Spanish, Korean, and Chinese. It is a good book, even if I was the instrument God used to write it.

That was several years ago. Many things have happened since that have given me a better understanding of the *real* purpose of prayer and what is really important. If you are looking for a formula that when carefully applied *may* cause God to grant all the things you desire, you have not found it. However, if you are in search of the truth that will develop confidence in your ability to pray effectually, this may be the book you need to read.

CHAPTER ONE

The Beginning of a National Prayer Movement

I was sitting in my office on a Saturday morning in January 1979 when I heard a voice in my spirit say, "I want you to call the nation to prayer." My first response was, "Lord, You need to talk to Billy Graham or Oral Roberts." I was the pastor of a small church in East Texas. I had only been there two years and in that time, we had experienced a tremendous revival. Over 500 people had confessed Jesus as Savior in the 22 months I had served that church. This revival came in response to the prayers of the people. At one point, we prayed for 90 days, and for the last 21 days, we prayed round the clock twenty-four hours a day.

In the 7 weeks following this concerted effort in prayer, we saw more than 400 souls come to Jesus. What a move of the Spirit that was! But now, God was saying,

"I want you to call the nation to prayer." I did not know how to do it. Surely, I would have to depend on God. He knew what to do better than I did. *God often calls the foolish ones to confound the wise and the weak to shut the mouths of the strong. He even calls those who are "nobodies" to do things that amaze the "somebodies."*

At any rate, I began that very day. In my head, I heard a radio broadcast—a fifteen-minute daily broadcast built around the idea of enlisting, instructing, encouraging, and inspiring God's people to pray. The program would begin with a tiffany roll of drums, a full orchestra, and a heavy voice singing "God of Our Fathers." I actually heard it in my spirit. The voice sounded like Tennessee Ernie Ford, so I went to look for the music but found nothing like what I had heard.

The very next day, I talked to a missionary speaker about the experience I had the day before. I told him about the music and asked if he knew of such a recording. He said no, but he was personally acquainted with one of the best-known writers and arrangers of music in the Christian world at the time. He suggested we give him a call, which we did. This well-known writer and composer personally answered the phone when we called. I described what I had heard and asked him if he knew of any such recording. He said no, but he was on his way to London the next day and would bring some of England's best musicians together for a recording session. He volunteered to write and produce the music I had described while he was there. In less than three weeks, I had a recording of "Faith of Our Fathers" done by some of the best musicians in Great Britain. What a miracle!

I had the music, now I needed the voice. As God would have it, I read an announcement in the newspaper that Big John Hall was going to be singing and ministering in a church in a town close by. When I saw the announcement, I knew the voice I had heard was John Hall's. I went to that service and was introduced to this wonderful brother in the Lord. I told him my vision and ask him to sing with the music I had in hand. He told me he had a recording studio in Dallas and would be glad to do the intro for the broadcast. He did a few days later.

If all this had been planned I am sure it would have taken months to bring it to pass. But brilliantly orchestrated by God, it took only three or four weeks. What divine intervention.

I have to confess that I prayed very little about any of these things. By that time, I had learned the secret of seeking God and His kingdom first and then confidently waiting for Him to do what I couldn't.

I had His word: *"All these things will be added unto you"* (Matthew 6:33). We do not have to beg God to assist us in doing what He has directed. That's a given. He will always equip us with the tools to do what He has commissioned. *Prayer is not the means by which we get God to do our will. It is the means by which we set up the appropriate grounds for His intervention.*

God is sovereign. He has the power and authority to step into and control any and all situations. However, He rarely does unless someone prays a prayer of faith in alignment with His will. What am I saying? Most everything is controlled by natural law. The final outcome of every matter will follow a course determined by these laws unless God intervenes. A man gets into a car after drinking enough alcohol to impair his judgment and slow his reflexes. When he reaches a curve that is too sharp to negotiate at the speed he is traveling, natural law determines his vehicle will leave the road. God has nothing to do with it. However, many have been miraculously spared from the disastrous effects of natural law because of the prayers of mothers or wives who caused God to intervene.

This concept may seem disturbing to those who believe God controls the outcome of every situation. However, those of us who pray see just how important it is for us to do so intelligently. By that I mean prayers that are directed by the Holy Spirit. Paul tells us the Holy Spirit knows the mind of God and makes intercessions for us, through us, according to the will of God (Romans 8:26).

Our Father knows everything. He is, to use a theological term, omniscient. This means God has never learned anything. He can't learn. If He could learn, it would imply He did not know. If God did not know He would not be omniscient. This being true, the most important thing about prayer is not that God hears us but that we hear Him. When I hear Him, align myself with His revealed will, and pray, I set up the conditions for divine intervention. As a result of those prayers, God interferes with the natural laws that would rule the outcome if He does not.

What I just said is worth repeating: the most important thing about prayer is not that God hears us, but that we hear Him. This is why I am spending less and less time talking to God. I used to talk a lot and listen little. Now, I talk little and listen a lot. In listening to His voice, we will hear Him speak. Some call this *revelation*. Revelation is the foundation of faith. When I know God's will, I can pray with confidence. This is one way we become *"workers together with God"* (2 Corinthians 6:1-3). God does not work through those with whom He has little or no relation.

When I was led to call the nation to prayer in 1979, little emphasis was placed on prayer, and so far as I knew, there was not one other national prayer movement. I found later that Intercessors for America was functioning but without a great deal of interest. Today, there are scores of national and international prayer ministries. Praise God, there are more people in America praying today than at any time in history. Millions are now committed to pray until revival comes. It will happen.

PRAYER

Heavenly Father, grant us the wisdom and patience to sit in Your presence.

Teach us to hold our tongues when we come before You. Set a guard at the door of my mouth. *"Let the words of my mouth and the meditations of my heart be acceptable in your sight, my Lord and my Redeemer"* (Psalm 19:14). I need to hear what You have to say, for You know all things. You know when someone is near to eternity. You can stop what is about to happen. You've done it many times in the past. Show us so we may pray intelligently (prayers led by the Spirit). Holy Spirit, enlighten our minds that we may pray the will of God. These things we pray. In Jesus' name. Amen!

CHAPTER TWO

Prayer's Primary Purpose

In Matthew 21:12, Jesus went into the temple and drove out those who were doing things contrary to the will of God. As He cleansed the temple, He said, *"It is written, My house shall be called a house of prayer."* Note carefully the setting and His words. First, let us observe He was in the temple Herod had recently completed. It sat on the foundation of the temple Solomon had built many years before. God has clearly identified the temple as His house in the words of Jesus: *"My house"* and has demonstrated by the demeanor of His Son how He felt about what was going on there.

In Solomon's prayer of dedication found in the book of 2 Chronicles, it was not so much the building that was dedicated to God but the place. His prayer was, *"When your people pray toward this place, hear them."* (2 Chronicles 6:21). It was a holy place because God made it holy. Although this was not the same building, it was the same place. In essence, what Jesus is saying is that His house, His dwelling place, shall be known as a house of prayer because that, in fact, is what it is. The place He has chosen to meet with His people shall be a house of prayer. Notice these words: *"but you have made it."* (Matthew 21:13). His house was what they had made it and what they had made it was not what God wanted it to be. The same is true today. His house is what we have made it.

I have traveled much of the world. I have visited and ministered in many different denominations. Sad to say, with a few exceptions, God's house is not a house of prayer. In regularly called services, more time is given to announcements than to prayer. The time given for receiving offerings is more than that given to prayer. Jesus did not say My house shall be a house of preaching, teaching, music, singing, or fellowship—as wonderful as these things may be. He said, *"My house shall be a house of prayer"* (Matthew 21:13). What we have made His house is not something bad. No, in fact, we have made it something good—good music, good fellowship, good preaching and teaching. The only thing wrong is we have not made His house what He has clearly established it to be. If it is His house, He has the right to say what He wants it to be. No one would argue with that conclusion. We have not, I am sorry to say, made it a house of prayer.

I have observed that in the regular services of the local church less than ninety seconds of a ninety-minute service are given to prayer. And quite often, this is only a perfunctory exercise with little meaning. Pastors and church leaders seem to feel that giving much time to prayer has a negative effect. Hence, prayer seems to be the least planned part of the service. Music is planned. Offerings are planned. Preaching is planned. What about prayer? Why is it not planned? Is it possible that our lack of faith in the effects of prayer causes such indifference?

Typically, we give priority to the things we deem most important. Perhaps this is why we give a lot of time to preaching. We feel this is the most important thing. It is important. However, if we want to follow the revealed will of God, we will make His house a house of prayer. These things concern the local church, which is often called the "house of God." Now, I want to bring the matter closer to home.

YOU ARE THE TEMPLE OF THE HOLY GHOST

When Jesus was on the earth, it was believed God dwelled in the temple in Jerusalem. The people of Israel went there to offer sacrifices and give offerings. It was the central meeting place. However, all that changed after Jesus died for our sins, was resurrected, and ascended to heaven where He offered His blood as atonement for our sins on the altar. There, He sat down. His first request of the Father was to send the Holy Spirit to live in the people for whom He died. One hundred and twenty of them were waiting in Jerusalem near the temple. They had been commanded by the Lord just before He left them, *"Do not leave Jerusalem until you are indued with power from on high"* (Acts 1:4). Earlier, He had said concerning the Holy Spirit, *"He is with you, but He shall be in you"* (John 14:17).

As those believers waited, Scripture says in Acts 2:1:

When the day of Pentecost had fully come they were all in one place and in one accord, when suddenly there came from heaven a sound like a mighty rushing wind and it filled all the house where they were sitting and they were all filled with the Holy Ghost and began to speak with other languages as the Spirit gave them to speak.

Solomon's temple or the temple mount would no longer be the house of God. After that, the church would be called the temple of the Holy Ghost and each member of that royal body would be seen as a temple of the Holy Ghost. Paul queries, *"Don't you know that you are the temple of the Holy Ghost?"* (1 Corinthians 3:16). This question was to be taken both in the corporate and individual sense. The corporate body is the temple, and God dwells in it in a special way, but we are also to be viewed as individual temples of God. Christ dwells in each of us. Both corporately and individually, we are the habitation of God through the Spirit (Ephesians 2:22, KJV). Now, it is the house in which you live that is to be a *"house of prayer."* And you are required to make it that.

WHO OWNS THE HOUSE?

This question must be answered before we go any further. The apostle Peter tells us we were purchased with a price, which is not silver or gold but the precious blood of Jesus: *"You were not redeemed with corruptible things, like silver or gold, from your aimless conduct received by tradition from your fathers, [19]but with the precious blood of Christ, as of a lamb without blemish and without spot"* (1 Peter 1:18).

The apostle Paul put it this way, *"You are not your own. You are the temple of God"* (I Corinthians 6:19). You live where you live by God's permission. It is not your house. You are not the owner. It is His house and He has the right to say what He wants it to be. We are tenants who live, by His permission, in a house that belongs to Him. The truth is He lives with us. Yes, Jesus lives with us; however, the house does not belong to us; it is His. As the owner, He has the authority to tell the tenant what He wants His house to be. Since we live in the house by His permission and do not pay rent, we should regard the wishes of the owner of the house.

Is there any doubt as to what He wants His house to be? The answer to this question is no, none at all. He said, "My house shall be a house of prayer." He expects us to make it that. Let me say it again, God expects you and me to make the house in which we live a house of prayer.

If the house in which you live is not a house of prayer, it is because you have failed to make it that. Would you agree? The house is what you make it. Perhaps, you will respond, "I have tried, but I just don't seem to be able to do it. I know it should be and I want it to be, but I just keep on failing." I know this is, or has been, the experience of many of God's children. They know God is their Father and want to have a relationship with Him but for some reason, they fail to break into the place of intimacy with Him. For many, prayer is not a meaningful experience to which they look forward.

Here are two suggestions to boost your prayer life and experience an intimate relationship with God:

1. Forget What You Have Been Taught about Prayer

First, you may need to forget a lot of what you have been taught about prayer. Most of the teaching we have heard and read about prayer has to do with us: our holiness, goodness, and righteousness. Will God hear sinners? Will God respond to failures? Will God hear a person whose faith is weak? Should I kneel when I pray? Do I have to pray out loud? Will God hear a thought prayer? To these questions I respond: prayer is not about us—it is about God. It is not so much about talking to God. It is about entering His presence and living with the awareness He is there all the time. Whether life is going well or you are in trouble, He said, *"I will never leave you. I will never forsake you… I will be with you always, even to the end of the ages"* (Hebrews 13:5-6, Matthew 28:20). What does this all mean? It means exactly what it says, no ifs, ands, or buts. We do not have to get His attention, we have it.

2. Know Who You Are

One of the big problems is that many are not sure they are welcome in God's presence. They are insecure about their relationship with Him. They still see themselves as sinners—not little sinners, big ones. Is that what God calls us? No, God calls us saints (holy ones) (Ephesians 1:1). Paul addresses his letter *"To the saints who are in Ephesus, and faithful in Christ Jesus."*

God calls us His children. Yet, we see ourselves as stepchildren. We know we are in the family but are not sure we really belong to Him or that He is, in fact, our Father.

To have a meaningful experience in prayer, we must know who we are. When we came into this world, we were all children of the first Adam. We were born in sin, as David put it, and shapen in iniquity (Psalm 51:5). We were condemned before we ever sinned because of who we were. We were children of the first Adam and had nothing to do with it. No one asked us if we wanted to be born. Suddenly, we appeared on the scene and didn't know how we got here. Some people have had such difficult lives they wished they had never been born.

In the first Adam, Scripture says we had no hope in this world. We were born with the sentence of death written on our birth certificates. The entire human race was under the same condemnation.

The creation waits in eager expectation for the sons of God to be revealed. [20]*For the creation was subjected to frustration, not by its own choice, but by the will of the one who subjected it, in hope* [21]*that the creation itself will be liberated from its bondage to decay and brought into the glorious freedom of the children of God.* (Romans 8:19, NIV)

But God had a plan to redeem man and bring him into full fellowship with Himself as one of His own sons. From the very beginning, God planned to make the fallen sons of Adam just like His only begotten Son Jesus, who is called the second Adam.

The first step in this process was establishing the law. Its purpose was to show mankind the legal grounds under which he was justly sentenced. The law was not given to give us hope. It came to increase condemnation (Romans 7:7). It did its work. The law was a part of God's plan. It also established legal grounds for a temporary reprieve from the just penalty for sin demanded by the law. This reprieve could be acquired by the offering of a sacrifice, which would push back the death sentence by one year. These offerings were made over and over, but they had no power to actually cleanse a person from the guilt of sin.

And every priest stands ministering daily and offering repeatedly the same sacrifices, which can never take away sins. 12But this Man, after He had offered one sacrifice for sins forever, sat down at the right hand of God, 13from that time waiting till His enemies are made His footstool. 14For by one offering He has perfected forever those who are being sanctified. (Hebrews 10:11-14)

There was never a moment in time or eternity when God thought of allowing mankind to live under these conditions forever. He had a purpose, a plan that the law with its sacrifices foreshadowed. But God also knew that in the process of time, the system would change. He would change it. That is exactly what happened when Jesus came into the world.

God so loved the world, that He sent His only begotten Son into the world that whosoever (anyone who ever) believes in Him should not perish but have eternal life." 17 "God did not send His son to condemn the world, but that the world, through him, might be saved. (John 3:16-17)

John 3:16 is often called the golden text of the Bible. And so it is. This is the good news the angels proclaimed at His birth. *"We bring you good tidings of great joy which shall be to all people, for unto you is born this day…a savior which is Christ the Lord"* (Luke 2:10-11).

These verses do not tell the complete story, but they say a lot. A new covenant was about to be shared with the entire human race, not just to Israel but also to the whole world, to all people, both Jew and Gentile. This covenant would not be based on the works of the law but on faith in the works of Christ Jesus. It would not be based on what we do for God but on what God through Christ Jesus did for us. God would open a door into His presence and with joyful anticipation wait for us to enter.

WHAT IS THIS GOOD NEWS?

Paul says in Romans 1:16-17: *"I am not ashamed of, nor will I ever hesitate to proclaim, the gospel, because in it Almighty God announces that deliverance from sin and its consequences is His gift to every person who only believes, including both Jews and Greeks."* Again, this is faith that leads to and is expressed in faithfulness to God our Savior and Jesus Christ our Lord. It is written, *"The just shall live by faith"* not by works of the law (Romans 1:17). Furthermore, a new truth is revealed about righteousness, which was earned by Jesus Christ through strict and perfect obedience to all of the demands of the law. Moreover, our Father credits this perfect righteousness to the account of all who believe.

It is my humble opinion that until we are able to grasp this truth, we will not have confidence in the presence of God. We must believe that we *have,* present tense, righteousness we did not earn through our own works. It is not righteousness that we attain but one we obtain by faith alone. When we have it, we are identified as the *"righteousness of God"* (1 Corinthians 5:21)

Many people believe they are loved but are not sure they are accepted. It is not possible to feel accepted and secure if we focus on our sins, failures, and shortcomings. We feel secure and accepted when we keep our eyes focused, not on ourselves, but on Jesus and the righteousness He earned. This righteousness came through perfect obedience to every demand of the law God credits to the account of all who have faith. The writer of the old gospel song said:

There was a time on earth,

When in the book of heaven,

An old account was written,

For sins yet unforgiven.

The old account was large,

And growing every day,

For I was always sinning

And never tried to pay.

My name was at the top

And a million things below

I went unto the keeper

And settled it long ago.

(Frank M. Graham)

It is a good old song, but I did not settle the account. Jesus did. It was marked paid in full when God the Father credited the righteousness earned by Jesus to my account. All I did was believe it, and it was done. However, if I believe that any part of the old account is still standing, I do not have the boldness necessary to stand in the presence of God.

Satan is the accuser of God's children. It is his business to turn our thoughts toward our imperfections. As long as he can do this, we will not have the confidence necessary to approach the throne of God whose word to us is *"Come boldly."* Come confidently, not trusting your goodness but Christ's goodness that purchased entrance into the very presence of God for us.

What is the good news? It is simply that God has provided a way for the sinful sons of Adam (who of their own volition have turned *"every man to his own ways"* — Isaiah 53:36) to be restored to fellowship with God and to reach their full potential as sons of God like Jesus. The good news is we are welcome in His presence. We can have fellowship with Him. We can talk to Him about our deepest needs.

SUMMARY

The primary purpose of prayer is to develop an intimate, meaningful relationship with God through on-going communication. This is possible because of the work of Christ on our behalf at the cross. Having been justified by faith in the work of Christ Jesus, we have peace with God and confidence to come into His presence. We can now have a meaningful relationship with the Father of us all, *"especially those who believe"* (1 Timothy 4:10).

PRAYER

Father, grant me the ability to focus my spiritual eyes on the finished work of Jesus. He obeyed every demand of the law. His holiness is perfect, and You have credited His righteousness to my account. His righteousness is sufficient. In Christ, I have kept the law, and You view me as You view Your only begotten Son. I can have a meaningful relationship with You because of Him.

CHAPTER THREE

A Philosophy of Prayer

But why would God want us to pray? That He does is evident throughout the Word. His invitation to come into His presence, to call upon Him, to ask, seek, and knock is a more than adequate basis for such a belief.

In one of his books, E.M. Bounds attributed the following quote to John Wesley: *"God does nothing but in answer to prayer."* I read this as a young preacher and for some reason believed it. This conviction has been the strength of my ministry for more than 60 years. Though I would not say God does *absolutely nothing* but in answer to prayer, I will say, as a rule, God does nothing but in answer to believing prayer.

PHILOSOPHY

Philosophy is not a bad word. *"Beware lest anyone cheat you through philosophy and empty deceit, according to the tradition of men, according to the basic principles of the world, and not according to Christ"* (Colossians 2:8). Philosophy that is according to the tradition of men, based on the principles of the world and not according to Christ is most certainly bad. However, philosophy based on the principles set forth in the Word of God and aligned with the Spirit of Jesus Christ is good. Science looks for facts. Philosophy wants to know why. Our Father is not disturbed by an honest inquiry along these lines. In my book, *Why Pray?* I dealt at length with this subject. For those who failed to read that book, I will give a brief synopsis.

Why would an omnipotent, omniscient God need us to pray? Can He not do what He wants to do without us? Is there something God lacks that we can contribute to Him, some insufficiency that we can supply through our prayers? Several years ago, I began to ask these questions. Frankly, I could not find the answers. I read many of the classics on prayer that were available at the time and found the majority of them said essentially the same things in different ways. They discussed various kinds of prayer, including the how-to of prayer, but none seemed to go into the "why."

As I analyzed my own prayers, I saw that most of what I was calling prayer was not prayer at all. As I listened to myself and others pray, I realized someone listening would get the impression God didn't know very much. Prayer seemed to be an informing session where I told God about things He had perhaps overlooked. Sometimes prayer was an instructing session where I told God how He should deal with certain matters. My prayers seemed to imply God would not know what to do unless He had my suggestions or directions. At other times, I prayed as if God wasn't as concerned about a matter as I thought He should be. It was my duty to somehow stir Him up to the point where His concern would, at least, equal mine. As these patterns became obvious, I realized that much of my prayer time was an exercise in futility.

To understand the underlying purpose of prayer, one must know how God implements His will in this universe. And to understand this, we must go back to the beginning. *"In the beginning, God created the heavens and the earth"* (Genesis 1:1). Paul tells us: *"By Him (Jesus) all things were created that are in heaven and that are on earth, visible and invisible, whether thrones or dominions or principalities or powers. All things were created through Him and for Him. And He is before all things, and in Him all things consist"* (Colossians 1:16, 17). Every part of the universe was created in perfect order and balance, sustained and held together by Christ. He did not create the fish before the water. First, the grass was created, then the cattle. God built into His creation an amazing interdependence. All living things depend upon other living things, and the whole community of living things has a corporate dependence on the environment. For a living thing to live a living thing, plant or animal, must die.

The universe God created is designed to function under a system of laws: natural, physical, and spiritual. Those who study such matters tell us there are multiplied billions of systems like our own Milky Way. Each has billions of stars orbiting the center of the universe. Every planet revolves around its gravitational pull and is held in its place—by law. Our God created it all. He operates within the very laws He established. He does not change the length of the days. He does not make decisions about the weather. Law determines those things. When warm, moisture-laden air meets a cool front, clouds will form, and precipitation will occur. There is nothing supernatural about it. All things are controlled by law. God will not displace or set aside these laws unless there are good reasons for doing so, even then, only in a very lawful and legal manner.

Until the sixth creative day, all was well and good. But on that day, as some view it, God created a potential problem:

Let Us make man in Our image, according to Our likeness; let them have dominion over the fish of the sea, over the birds of the air, and over the cattle, over all the earth and over every creeping thing that creeps on the earth." So God created man in His own image; in the image of God He created him; male and female He created them." Then God blessed them, and God said to them, "Be fruitful and multiply; fill the earth and subdue it; have dominion over the fish of the sea, over the birds of the air, and over every living thing that moves on the earth. (Genesis 1:26-28)

When God created man and woman and placed them upon the earth, He gave them dominion over every living thing, including the serpent. Though we do not find anywhere in the Word that man was given "free will," we believe he was because of the way God dealt with him. Genesis 2:16 shows that Adam was given the right to decide whether or not he would obey God's command. He was not forced to obey or to disobey. Being innocent, he had no more inclination to disobey than to obey. The choice was his; he had the option to obey or disobey. However, knowing what Adam would do, God gave him a warning of the awful consequences if he chose to disobey. Genesis 3:1-6 tells the story of the bad choice Adam made. The rest of the Bible records the terrible results and ultimate resolution of the consequences of that decision.

[1]Now the serpent was more crafty than any of the wild animals the LORD God had made. He said to the woman,

"Did God really say, 'You must not eat from any tree in the garden'?"

2The woman said to the serpent, "We may eat fruit from the trees in the garden, 3but God did say, 'You must not eat fruit from the tree that is in the middle of the garden, and you must not touch it, or you will die.'"

4"You will not surely die," the serpent said to the woman. 5"For God knows that when you eat of it your eyes will be opened, and you will be like God, knowing good and evil."

6When the woman saw that the fruit of the tree was good for food and pleasing to the eye, and also desirable for gaining wisdom, she took some and ate it. She also gave some to her husband, who was with her, and he ate it. 7Then the eyes of both of them were opened, and they realized they were naked. (Genesis 3:1-6)

Adam's decision did not catch God off guard. He who knows all knew what Adam would do, but his disobedience did present a problem. How could a sovereign God in a universe governed by natural law and a world system under the dominion of a rebel to whom He gave free will, exercise His will? If God had imposed His will on man, man would not have been free. On the other hand, if God had no legal way to impose His will, He would not be sovereign.

Early on in the history of Christianity, theologians questioned how God can be truly sovereign and man truly free. Unable to find an answer that satisfied a majority, the church divided into two camps. One division followed Jacobus Armenias and the other John Calvin. Those who held the view that God is sovereign; therefore, man could not be truly free were called Calvinist. Those who emphasized the "free will" position were called Armenians. These students of theology could not resolve the seeming conflict between God's sovereignty and man's freedom. Their reasoning led them to the conclusion that if God is sovereign, man cannot be free. On the other hand, if man is free, God cannot be sovereign.

With the greatest respect for Calvin and Armenias (noted scholars who have made so many positive contributions to the cause of Christ), I must, with genuine humility say, it is my conviction that God is sovereign and man is free. In fact, I believe it was for this very reason God established what I have come to view as the highest law of the universe—a law that protects both His sovereignty and man's free will.

LESSER AND HIGHER LAWS

The law of gravity is a high law but not the highest. Every day, people get on airplanes that weigh as much as 600,000 pounds or more. By using the power of its engines to give it thrust, that huge hunk of metal is pushed down the runway at ever-increasing speeds until its wings lift it off the tarmac. It literally soars upward until it reaches its assigned altitude. Then it levels out and flies across the earth at some 500 miles per hour, not once breaking the law of gravity. All the time, gravity is trying to force it back to the ground but is unable to do so because a higher law is in force. Velocity overcomes gravity. As the pilot gently reduces the speed, the law of gravity pushes the plane back to the earth.

A longstanding conviction of mine is that prayer is a spiritual law. I believe when it is implemented properly with faith, it permits God to lawfully exercise His sovereignty in a universe controlled by natural laws and a world system under the dominion of a rebel to whom God has given free will.

From the beginning, those among the rebels have chosen, of their own free will, to obey God. As they pray on the earth what God wills in heaven, they set up the appropriate conditions for divine intervention even when doing so overrides the free will of man.

EXAMPLE

Pharaoh did not want to release the people of Israel. It was not his will to do so. It was, however, the will of God. As the people prayed, the Lord sent a deliverer, Moses, who led the Israelites out of Egypt. After seeing the hand of God manifest through Moses and the firstborn of Egypt dead, Pharaoh was willing to let the Israelites go. Later, he changed his mind and set out with his army in hot pursuit. The Red sea opened as Moses communed with God and the people walked across on dry ground. Pharaoh presumed he could follow; however, in response to the prayers of Moses and the people of God, he and his army were drowned in the sea—*against their will*, I might add. When we pray the will of God we set up legal grounds for a miracle. I am not saying miracles are guaranteed through our prayers. Rather, I am saying we make it possible.

The book of Joshua records the story of the Israelites possessing the land God promised Abraham as an eternal inheritance. During one fierce battle with the Amorites, they needed more daylight to complete the route. As Joshua consulted with the Lord about the matter, evidently, he was told what to do. Joshua came out of the place of prayer and commanded the sun to stand still. It did—for almost a full day according to Joshua 10:13. Through prayer, Joshua determined the will of God about the matter. He was told what to do; he did it, and the battle was won. He made it lawful for God to temporarily set aside the natural law and do what was necessary to extend the length of a day. This happened because a man, Joshua, knew God's will concerning the matter and through prayer, set up the appropriate conditions for a miracle.

Do you think you need a longer day? Don't try it. Joshua did not come up with a bright idea and then ask God to make it work. He got the idea from God. When God tells us to do something, it will be successful, not once in a while but every time. I am not implying there will be no problems. The truth is there may be many problems.

Moses was in the will of God when he went to deliver Israel from Egyptian bondage, but it was not an easy task. At times, it looked as if the entire idea was a mistake. Just when it seemed they had finally been released and were on their way to the Promised Land, Pharaoh changed his mind and led his army in pursuit. Behind were Pharaoh and his army; ahead was the Red Sea. It seemed there was no way out. Something supernatural would have to happen. And it did.

Moses was a pray-er. He was always talking to God, and God was always talking to him. This time, the situation was desperate. They needed a miracle, but not once did Moses tell God what He should do. Moses spoke to the people who were already complaining: *"Do not be afraid. Stand still, and see the salvation of the Lord, which He will accomplish for you today. For the Egyptians whom you see today, you shall see again no more forever"* (Exodus 14:13). Then the Lord told Moses what to do: *"Lift up your rod, and stretch out your hand over the sea and divide it"* (Exodus 14:16). That he did, and the waters parted allowing the whole nation to cross on dry land. Moses' prayer and faith set up the conditions for God to do what He wanted. It is not clear whether or not Moses knew exactly what God was going to do, but he knew God would do something.

The prayer of faith makes it possible for God to do what He wills to do.

Prayer does not generally change the mind of God, though there have been times when He has changed His stated intention (see next chapter). Please don't get twisted out of shape by what may seem to make God helpless until we pray. Simply put, I am saying God is willing to wait for us to pray before He acts. Our faith and prayers seem to activate the promises of God. The promise of God is there, and He is ready to bring it to pass. But He is willing to wait until we, through prayer, activate it.

I was conducting a prayer conference in a Presbyterian church in Western Kansas several years ago. Following the morning service, a brother asked me to go with him for a drive, which I was glad to do. As we drove along, he told me the following story. He said. "I am a corn farmer and when we plant our corn. we buy insurance to protect the bank which loans us money for seed, and to cover our profit in case hail comes at the wrong time of the year. This spring" he continued, "I felt led to take a portion of the money I would use to buy insurance and give it to missions. Insurance costs about $40,000 per year, so I gave half of the money to missions and with the other half, I covered my loan at the bank."

By this time, we were traveling along a country road where there were fields of corn on both sides. I noticed they had really taken a beating from the hail. We were soon in a section, which looked altogether different. The brother said as he pointed, "That is my field. See what God has done in response to this step of faith." It was obvious there had been no hail on that field. Then he said, "I don't know if I will ever do this again, but I did it this time and God protected my crop." Crops had been hailed out all around, but not on this brother's land. Faith and prayer had set up the appropriate conditions for a miracle. Our Father likes to bless those who want to do His work. If this brother had selfish motives, I doubt the results would have been the same.

THE "IF" FACTOR

You may ask, "Do you think I could change the weather if I pray?" My answer would be probably not. However, "if" it is something that will bring glory to God and is a part of His plan, it will be done as we pray. You must understand the "if" factor that is always there. God cannot answer every prayer we pray. Not because He does not have the power or ability, but because it is not His will. Nowhere has God promised to answer every prayer. Things would be in a real mess if He did.

Garth Brooks recorded a song some time ago entitled, "Thank God for Unanswered Prayer." The song told the story of a young man who, while in high school was attracted to a girl he wanted more than anything. He prayed, "God give me that girl." At the time, he thought he just couldn't live without her. Twenty-five years later, at their class reunion, he saw her and responded: "Thank God for unanswered prayer."

Someone suggested that sometimes in response to prayer, God says "no." At other times, He says "Grow." Then there are times when He says "slow." Don't get in a hurry; wait. Other times, He says "Go." The coast is clear; go ahead. God can change the weather in answer to the prayers of His people. The skeptics may not believe it, but He has done it in the past and will do it in the future.

While in Florida, I heard the story of a hurricane that had been heading toward Miami. It was a big one, and if it hit, there was certainly going to be much damage and possibly loss of life. As it neared the coast, many Christians gathered and prayed that the course of the hurricane would be altered. Suddenly, it stopped and remained in the same place for hours as if gathering momentum for an attack. The people kept praying; it was almost as if a battle was going on. Then eventually, the hurricane moved but not toward the coast. It went to the northeast without causing any serious trouble. Did prayer change things? Indeed. It set up the conditions under which God could legally alter the course of the storm. Is this something that I can prove to an unbeliever? No, I can only report the facts. Every person has to choose for himself what he will believe. The facts are there was a hurricane headed for the coast of Florida; people prayed; the hurricane stopped, changed its course, and blew itself out. These are the facts. Believe what you like. As I grasped this principle, I understood certain Scriptures that had previously made little sense.

ONE OTHER SCRIPTURAL
EXAMPLE OF THIS PRINCIPLE

In Ezekiel Chapter 36, we have a clear example of this truth. Israel's national prophet speaking in God's behalf says to the nation: *"I will take you from among the nations, gather you out of all countries, and bring you into your own land. Then I will sprinkle clean water on you, and you shall be clean; I will cleanse you from all your filthiness and from all your idols. I will give you a new heart and put a new spirit within you"* (Ezekiel 36:24-26). After reemphasizing those words, God says, *"I, the Lord, have spoken it, and I will do it"* (Ezekiel 36:36). That is where most of us stop reading, but look at the next verse: *"I will also let the house of Israel inquire of Me to do this for them."* God, through His prophet, said He would do these things, but He required the people to ask.

The same principle is found in the book of James: *"You do not have because you do not ask"* (James 4:2). We must pray; it is the only way God can legally intervene. What I have tried to show in this teaching is that God operates by divine laws and established principles. He exercises His will under strict rules and has chosen to involve us in that process. That is exciting! We are not pawns on some great chessboard of life to be moved about by forces over which we have no control. We are involved. We are working together with God in the implementation of His holy will. Get these truths in your spirit and your attitude toward life will change. You can make a difference; you can set up the conditions under which things can be changed.

I agree that it doesn't make sense—unless you understand how God implements His will.

As stated earlier, two hundred years ago, John Wesley said, "God does nothing but in answer to prayer." Wesley didn't give any further explanation of that statement, and I believed it for years before I understood it. God must wait until He is asked before He can do what He wants to do—not because He is powerless, but because of the way He has chosen to exercise His will.

Recently, I read the story of Pastor Wentworth Pike who went into his office to pray on a Sunday afternoon for the evening service.

As he was praying, he felt a strong compulsion to pray that someone would be saved in the evening service. Furthermore, Pastor Pike said, "I felt that the prayer should not be merely that some person would be saved but that there was a particular person for whom the request was to be made, but I knew not whom." As he reasoned about the matter, he thought, if God desired him to pray about a particular person, He should tell him who that person was. So he asked who is it, Lord? God did not give him the name of the person but simply told him to pray, which he did. At first, he prayed for several whom he knew were not saved, calling their names out to God, but the compulsion did not cease. The voice within kept saying, "I want you to intercede for that one I want to save in the service tonight!" This was incredible. Nothing like this had ever happened to him before. In fact, he was not given to voices or dreams and did not expect any, but the compulsion continued.

So he went for a walk, thinking that perhaps he was overworked and imagining things. Upon returning to his office, the heavy inner conviction was still there, so he prayed: "Lord, I believe there is one particular unsaved person you want to bring to yourself in tonight's service. I don't know who it is…but save this soul tonight. Bring him or her under deep conviction."

Before the service began, he met with a group of men to pray. Not knowing if he should share the experience he had just gone through, he heard himself blurting it out. One of the men began to pray, "Lord, you know this person You have laid upon our pastor's heart. Save him tonight, Lord."

When Pastor Pike walked through the doorway near the platform, he looked back and saw a man and a little girl coming through the main entrance. Not knowing exactly how to proceed, he extended his hand to the man and said, "Good evening, I'm Wentworth Pike, the pastor." The man replied, "Can I join your church?"

Pastor Pike responded, "I am not sure that joining the church is what you need. Sit over there and get acquainted until the service begins."

"I don't know what it is I need, but I know I need to get right with God." The man listened carefully as the message of salvation was presented. When the invitation was given, he immediately responded and received Jesus Christ as Savior. After prayer, he stood before the congregation and told the following story: "About two o'clock this afternoon, a strange thing happened. My little girl and I were at home alone. I was reading the Sunday comics to her when the strangest feeling came over me. I just knew that I had to get right with God. I put the paper down and said, 'Come on honey, let's go for a ride.'

"I didn't know where to go for help. The only place I could think of was a little church out in the community where I went a few times as a boy. When we got there, the grass in the yard was knee-high and there were boards on the windows. Just then, a man came down the road and I ask him whether there would be a service there tonight.

'No,' he said. 'That church has been closed for ten years.'

So we just got back into the car and drove around, but I couldn't get rid of the feeling I had to get right with God.

"As I drove back into town, I came down this street (I had never driven through this part of town before) and noticed the sign in front of your church. Somehow, I just knew that this was the place where I was going to find the answer. When I came in, the pastor talked to me and showed me from the Bible that what I needed was to be saved. His sermon made it all so plain, so I received Jesus as my Savior and that awful feeling I had all afternoon is gone."

Pastor Pike, in responding to the urge to pray had set up the appropriate conditions for the miraculous salvation of this dear man.

PRAYER

Father, help us to hear, be obedient to the compulsion to pray and keep on praying until the answer comes. Father, more than anything, we want Your kingdom to come, and Your will to be done on the earth as it is in heaven. I know You have a will for my life and family. You have a will for my church, city, state, and nation.

You have a will for the kingdoms of this world. You said a time will come when the kingdoms of this world shall become the kingdom of the Lord and of His Christ. Let it be, Lord Jesus. May Your will be done in this matter. Amen!

CHAPTER FOUR

The Listening Part of Prayer

A meaningful conversation must have two sides; one speaks; the other listens. Prayer also has two sides. I speak to God and listen for His response. In the early part of my prayer life, I did most of the talking; now, I do most of the listening. It is much more important for us to hear what the Lord is saying than for Him to hear what we are saying. He really doesn't need to listen to us because He already knows what we need before we ask (Matthew 6:8) and has committed Himself to meet all of our needs according to His riches in glory (Philippians 3:19). This being true, listening would seem to be much more important than speaking. Having said this, I will share a couple of my personal experiences. One of these experiences came at an early point in my ministry.

I was serving at a small church in Southern Missouri as a pastor. One afternoon while kneeling at the front of the church in prayer, I was suddenly aware of the presence of the Lord Jesus. It seemed He was standing just to the left of where I was kneeling. His presence was so real I was afraid to look, knowing if I actually saw Him, I would die right there. I had been praying about a particular matter. I remember not what, but I recall praying, "Lord, I would like You to do this (I do not remember what), but I do not feel worthy." It was at that moment I heard Jesus say, "Son, whatever gave you the idea that I bless you because you are good. I bless you because I am good." What a revelation! It changed the way I thought about many things. Suddenly, I knew I was not saved because I was good; I was saved because God is good. I knew I was not to ever focus on my worthiness when I prayed but on God's goodness, love, and mercy. *"It was while we were yet sinners that Christ died for us"* (Romans 5:8).

A major problem for many of us who are now Christians by God's grace is the belief that God loves sinners and accepts them just as they are. However, once they are saved, He will have fellowship with them only when they do right. This feeling of unworthiness may be the reason many feel they do not or cannot hear from God. They continue to view themselves as sinners.

They forget that Christ Jesus came into the world to save sinners:

While yet sinners we were justified (declared, not guilty) by God the Father, the righteous judge of the whole earth. This, He could do, because an adequate offering for our sins was made by His son, Jesus. Through faith we personally activate all that Christ did in our behalf. Now, we who are saved are being made holy through the Word of God and by the continuing work of the Holy Spirit in our lives.

We are saved because of God's goodness. What a revelation! All of my understanding of God's great love began when I heard Him speak to me. I was praying when it happened. Yes, I was talking to God, but He broke into my volume of words with a few of His words that changed my life. I remember having heard someone say, "I think God is trying to tell me something." My response was, "God is not trying to do anything. When He wants you to hear, you will hear."

The most important thing for us to do when we pray is to have our spiritual ears tuned in to Him. It might be good to say, "Father, I humbly request that You interrupt me at any point in this prayer. I want to hear You."

I believe I can truthfully say that every life-changing revelation I have ever received from God came as I was praying and/or listening. A few days ago, I was listening to a recording of a teaching given by Dr. J. Sidlow Baxter at the University Baptist Church in Fayetteville, Arkansas. I was driving along listening carefully to the words of this sainted man of God, when I was suddenly smitten with conviction by the Holy Spirit. Let me explain. When God speaks, one may not actually hear a voice. In fact, that is rarely the case. It is usually an impression that comes to mind. God used the words of Dr. Baxter to get a message through to me. Right away I knew something I had not known before. It was not what was said but the thought that was triggered by what was said.

I knew something about myself I did not know before. As I evaluated my actions and attitudes throughout my life, I was convicted that much of what I had done was not to please God but to please others or myself. I had tried to live a good life, to be a man of integrity and honor. I have been faithful to my wife. I supported my family, paid my bills, etc., but why? As I thought about it, I realized, I had been much more concerned about how people would value me than what God thought of me. I did not like what I was seeing. I found myself in tears repenting of the sins of selfishness, self-centeredness, and a self-serving attitude.

Why do you go to church? Do you go to please God or are you going because of what you think someone might think about you if you didn't? Why do you obey the law? Do you obey because all authority is from God, and He has ordained law, yes, even the laws of the land? Do you have respect for these laws and keep them as unto God or because of the consequences you might experience by standing before an earthly judge? Are you trying to maintain *your reputation* or more interested in pleasing God? These are questions I had to face, and I did not like my score on the test.

God is not looking for a reason to condemn. He wants to help us become better than we are. He is working to make us exactly like His only begotten Son Jesus. He alone has the wisdom, power, patience, and commitment to fully accomplish what He has purposed. Keep your spiritual ears clean. Don't allow them to be filled with the noise of the world, as pleasant as it may be to the outer man. Let the inner man grow-up in Christ Jesus. As your goal in life, be determined to do all things in the name of Jesus and for the glory of God. Do not be discouraged when you fail. Cry out to your Father. He is kind and compassionate. He will comfort you with words of loving care.

Don't forget to listen for His voice. Jesus said, *"My sheep, know my voice...they come at my call."* Sheep do not understand everything the shepherd says, but they know the sound of His voice. You may not always understand what your Shepherd is saying, but His voice brings peace and security. Stay in the fold; don't run away, but if for some reason you do, know that He will seek you until He finds you and when He does, He will rejoice. Each and every sheep is valuable to the Shepherd, not just the ninety-nine in the fold but also the one that is lost.

PRAYER

Dear Father, give us ears to hear. It is not so important that You hear us but that we hear You. May we have ears like Samuel, who as a child said, "Speak, Lord because your servant hears." This is what I say today: "Speak Lord, my ears are open to Your word. I want to know and do what You want me to do." I know if I want You to hear me, I need to hear You. Open my ears; anoint them with ear salve. I do not want to be as those who have ears but cannot (because they will not) hear. Amen!

CHAPTER FIVE

More About the Relationship Part

If what I have said thus far is true, the primary purpose of prayer has little to do with us. It is all about God. He is the One who has saved us. He has opened a way into His presence through the righteousness of Christ and credited it to the account of those who have put their faith in Him. To these He has issued an invitation to come boldly into heaven's throne room.

Many, because of personal failures, are intimidated by the thought of coming into the presence of the Holy God. Think with me; we have been urged to come boldly into God's presence. Come with confidence. How can I do this? I come with a personal invitation, issued by the King of kings to visit Him at His throne. He has said, *"Let your requests be known"* (Philippians 4:6). *"Call unto me and I will answer"* (Jeremiah 33:3). *"Ask and you shall receive"* (Luke 11:9).

God wants to meet all our needs, but He also wants to have an intimate relationship with us. Why? He loves us. The human mind cannot comprehend certain things. Paul said, "I want you to know the unknowable" (Ephesians 3:19). I want you to comprehend that which cannot be comprehended, which is the love of God. God, our heavenly Father wants to have a meaningful relationship with us because He loves us.

A meaningful relationship is the product of meaningful communication.

There can be no such thing as a meaningful relationship apart from meaningful communication. This applies to both horizontal and vertical relationships. Notice what happens when we begin to draw near to God:

1. God begins to speak to us as we speak to Him.

2. He reveals His will to His friends.

3. Revelation becomes the foundation upon which faith is built.

4. A level of trust develops. His will and ways become important to us.

We see this is the record of Abraham's walk with God. Over and over we read: Abraham pitched his tent and built an altar. God was a vital part of His life. He was called, "*the friend of God*" (James 2:23). They walked and talked together. So when the wickedness of Sodom and Gomorrah became so great that the righteous Judge of the whole earth was forced to act, he could not or would not do so without telling His friend of His intentions. Why? Abraham had a nephew in Sodom and Gomorrah. God would not send judgment upon the place where Abraham's nephew lived without first telling His friend Abraham. The law required that judgment fall upon those wicked cities, but Abraham had to be told first because he had an interest there.

Immediately, Abraham interceded for those cities, not that he cared about them, but he was concerned about his nephew. Notice God did not quit answering until Abraham quit praying, even then God pulled Lot, his wife, and his children from the fire of destruction. Would you like to have that kind of relationship with God? Of course, you would, and you can have it.

Believe the Father wants to have a meaningful relationship with you. Believe His invitation to come into His presence includes you. Why not ask Him? Father, does this invitation to come boldly into Your presence include me? Yes, my son/daughter, anyone who hears may come.

"Anyone who is thirsty may come and partake of the water of life freely" (Revelation 22:17).

Are you thirsty? The Father says, *"Come!"* (Isaiah 55:1). You are welcome. Perhaps you are saying, "I am such a failure. I have wasted what God has given me. I am not worthy to come into His presence." Scripture records the story of the Prodigal Son who was saying the same thing. However, one day, he made up his mind to return to His Father. Even though he had not received an invitation, he said, *"I will return, and I will say, 'Father I have sinned against heaven and before you and am not worth to be called your son'"* (Luke 15:21). His father saw him a long way down the road and ran to meet him. With tears of joy, he recognized him as His son and fully restored him to a place at His table (Luke 15:11-32).

Our Father is waiting for us. Do not hesitate. You are welcome in the presence of the Lord. He wants to have a relationship with you. You can't fix yourself. He is ready to receive you just as you are, even if you are a prodigal. Not all prodigals have ended up in the pigsty. Many attend church every Sunday but have little or no relationship with the Father. Is this because the Father has rejected His child? Nay, dear one, never in a million years. Your Father waits. He will not force you into a relationship. He will wait for you to *"Draw near to Him."* When you do *"He will draw near to you"* (James 4:8). We have His Word in which His heart of love is revealed.

Prayer, at its best, is communion with God. We speak to Him and He speaks to us most often through His Word and in our focused thoughts as we talk to Him. He also communicates with us through impressions received from the Spirit in the words of fellow Christians. More often, our pastors bring words from God. It has been said, "I know that was only a man speaking, but God said something to me through him." Listen, God is still speaking to those who are listening. I have come to believe that half of our prayer time, if not more, should be spent listening.

Are you saying, "I used to hear from God but not anymore"? This seems to be the plight of many. What happened? In my humble opinion, God rarely continues to speak to those who have heard from Him and refuse or neglect to respond. Go back to the last word you believe you received from God. Did you respond appropriately? If not, that would be a good place to re-establish your relationship with Him.

TWO KINDS OF COMMUNICATION

My dear wife Velma and I have been married for 66 years, and I can truthfully say I have never raised my voice to speak to her in an unkind way, nor has she to me in all those years. At times, I was silent but all the time communicating non-verbally something was wrong. You do not have to speak to say things. Jesus taught, not only by the words He spoke but also by the things He did. When He looked at Peter as the rooster crowed on that infamous day of His crucifixion, their eyes met, and Jesus said, "Peter, I love you." Peter's heart was broken; he went out and wept bitterly because of his weakness.

Jesus' look was not one of condemnation but of compassion and genuine concern for Peter. He failed but was full of godly sorrow. It worked repentance and he received forgiveness. After the resurrection, Jesus says: "Go tell my disciples and Peter that I am risen" (Mark 16:7). Peter, the one who had publicly denied Jesus received personal recognition. Jesus and Peter had a relationship that would not be broken by his failure. We can have the same kind of relationship with our Lord. He is not looking for a reason to end the relationship. His promise is, *"I will never leave you or forsake you; I will be with you always"* (Hebrews 13:5, Matthew 28:20). We have His word. We may fail, but He will never fail. Our faith may weaken, but His faithfulness is strong and His commitment to us is unbreakable. Will He hear if we pray? Yes, and He will answer when He can.

WHEN HE CAN? IS THERE ANY QUESTION ABOUT THIS?

The truth is God cannot always answer our prayers, not because He lacks the power to do so, but because it would not be in the best interest of the kingdom or ours. We do not always know what we need. He knows and is committed to meet all of our needs according to His wealth in glory (Philippians 4:19). This is His promise to those who believe. Needs, wants, and desires are not always the same. God will meet all the needs of His children, whether they are good or bad. It will rain on the just as well as the unjust. We all receive certain blessings whether we are saints or sinners. However, our Father is not stingy. He loves His children and will often bless us with gifts we have never asked for.

One morning, I drove into the parking lot of the church where I led an early morning prayer meeting. Sitting in my clearly marked parking place was a car. At 5:00 in the morning, parking places are not hard to find, so I took another place, went into the prayer meeting, and did what I was used to doing. When I came out to leave the church, the car was still in my parking space. By then, it was brighter outside, so I could see the car was a brand new Lincoln Town. As I was about to go around it to my car, a man came up, handed me the keys to the Lincoln and said, *"God told me to give you this car.*" It was, indeed, a new car with all the bells and whistles—a wonderful car, all paid for.

I had never prayed for a Lincoln Town Car, but I had a secret desire for one. God had met that secret desire because He wanted to surprise me. It was one of the few cars I ever owned that was not mortgaged. David said in Psalm 37:4, if we walk uprightly before God, He will give us the desires of our hearts, our secret desires. Never once in my life had I prayed for a Lincoln Town car. In fact, I didn't need a car. I had two cars at the time. God was meeting a desire, not a need in my life.

Work on your relationship with God. Let this become your primary objective in prayer.

PRAYER

Father this is my desire. I want to know You. I want to have an intimate relationship with You. I want the kind of relationship that would cause You to want to share Your heart with me. I want to know Your heart in order to come into agreement with You about Your plans for the future. I want to pray Your will, so You may do what You want to do. Amen.

WHY DID GOD CREATE US?

I was in my prayer place one morning when I heard the Lord say: "Son, anything I can do with you I can do without you." He paused for just a moment and said, "I don't need you. I want you." What a revelation. God, my Father, was saying to me, "I don't need you." Suddenly, I knew He did not need any of us. He did not create us because He had a need that we could meet. God is self-sufficient. He has no needs. If He did, He could meet them. God did not create us to serve Him. He doesn't need service. God did not create us to worship Him. He does not need worship. He is not discouraged. He does not need to be pumped up. God does not need you or me. He wants us.

I thought about these things all day, and the next morning I remember saying: "God, I know you did not create us because you had a need for us, so why did you create us?" Immediately, my mind went to Revelations 4:8-11:

> *8The four living creatures, each having six wings, were full of eyes around and within. And they do not rest day or night, saying: "Holy, holy, holy, Lord God Almighty, Who was and is and is to come!" 9Whenever the living creatures give glory and honor and thanks to Him who sits on the throne, who lives forever and ever, 10the twenty-four elders fall down before Him who sits on the*

throne and worship Him who lives forever and ever, and cast their crowns before the throne, saying: 11"You are worthy, O Lord, To receive glory and honor and power; for You created all things, And for your pleasure they were created.

There it was written clearly on the pages of God's Holy Word. God created us for His own good pleasure and only because He wanted to do so. He would create a race of intelligent beings who would of their own free will choose to have a relationship with Him. Free will is absolutely essential to a meaningful relationship. Man must be free to choose of his own volition to have a relationship with His heavenly Father. This whole process would be made more difficult because of the influence of the serpent.

Adam was created pure in every way. He was completely innocent with no more inclination to do wrong than to do right, to disobey than to obey. He was faced with only one prohibition: *"Of the tree in the midst of the garden you shall not eat. If you do you will die, the very same day"* (Genesis 3:3). Scripture records that Adam and his wife, Eve, disobeyed God, ate of the forbidden fruit and were banished from the garden and intimate fellowship with God. Innocence: freedom from guilt was the basis of fellowship with God. Adam lost his innocence through willful transgression. This resulted in the loss of fellowship with God.

The Bible contains the story of God's plan to restore fellowship with Adam's children who all died because of the federal head of the family. We all sinned in Adam, were declared guilty, and sentenced to eternal separation from God. But God, for His own good pleasure, sent a second Adam, His only begotten Son to regain, through perfect obedience, what the first Adam lost through disobedience.

Through the birth, obedience, death, resurrection, and ascension of Jesus to the throne of God, Christ Jesus established conditions for intimate relationships between God and man. At the throne of God, He offered His own blood as atonement for the sin of Adam and his descendants on the altar in the heavenly temple.

"But when this priest had offered for all time one sacrifice for sins, he sat down at the right hand of God. 13Since that time he waits for his enemies to be made his footstool, 14because by one sacrifice he has made perfect forever those who are being made holy" (Hebrews 10:12-14).

"Therefore, having been justified by faith, we have peace with God through our Lord Jesus Christ, 2through whom also we have access by faith into this grace in which we stand, and rejoice in hope of the glory of God" (Romans 5:1-2).

God created us for His own pleasure. My next question is, "Then, what do we do that brings You pleasure?" To my amazement, He answered, "Anything you do in My name to bring Me glory, anything you do to the best of your ability, anything that is right and helps people, pleases Me." As I heard these things, I seemed to catch a glimpse of the whole world. I could see the advancements in science, medicine, transportation, communications, arts, and architecture. It seemed to me that God was saying look at what I have created. Look at what man has accomplished. Look at all the good he has done. Suddenly, I knew God can be pleased with what a person does but not with the person and that imperfect people can accomplish great things. Bad people can do good things and good people can, at times, do bad things. I knew that even though not all works are equally important, any work could please God if done with the right motive, which is to bring pleasure to God.

God does not view things as sacred or secular. These are human designations; they are not scriptural. Every undertaking is sacred if done for the glory of God whether it is mowing the lawn, washing the car, painting the house, cleaning out the garage, teaching a Sunday school class, singing in the choir of the church, or playing an instrument. In Matthew 25:31-37, we find the record of words attributed to Jesus:

31When the Son of Man comes in His glory, and all the ⌐holy angels with Him, then He will sit on the throne of His glory. 32All the nations will be gathered before Him, and He will separate them one from another, as a shepherd divides his sheep from the goats. 33And He will set the sheep on His right hand, but the goats on the left. 34Then the King will say to those on His right hand, 'Come, you blessed of My Father, inherit the kingdom prepared for you from the foundation of the world: 35for I was hungry and you gave Me food; I was thirsty and you gave Me drink; I was a stranger and you took Me in; 36I was naked and you clothed Me; I was sick and you visited Me; I was in prison and you came to Me.'

37"Then the righteous will answer Him, saying, 'Lord, when did we see You hungry and feed you,

Or thirsty and give you drink. When did we see you in prison and visit you." Jesus answered, "In as much as you did it onto one of the least of these my brethren, you did it to Me.'

The response of those who heard these words of the King is interesting. They seem to have been surprised they had done anything that would have been noticed by the King. Their response was: "When did we do this, Lord? We didn't know You were watching. We were just doing what seemed right." When we stand before

God, we may learn that what we did without fanfare or notice counted most.

God doesn't need us. He wants us because He loves us. He didn't have to create us, but He did because He wanted to. It is not service He wants from us; it is a relationship.

PRAYER

Father, help us to live our lives to bring You pleasure. May all we do reflect our knowledge of the fact that we are Yours in both the creative and redemptive sense. You purchased us with the blood of Your only begotten Son. We are Yours; do with us as You please. We surrender our all to You. You are our rightful owner. Father, we love and trust You. Amen!

CHAPTER SIX

Prayer and the Harvest

In Matthew 9:38 when Jesus saw the multitudes, He was moved with compassion. In the Greek, this word means to hurt inside. When Jesus saw the multitude of people, He was filled with emotions that caused him to hurt inside. He saw them as they really were: sheep not having a shepherd, no one to lead, feed, and protect them. With no sense of direction, they were scattered. He hurt for them. It was at that moment Jesus spoke these words to His disciples. *"The harvest is truly great, but the laborers are few"* (Matthew 9:36, 37). There can be no harvest without laborers. Who wants to be a laborer? We want to be leaders, to have followers, but who wants to be a laborer?

These days, we have one leadership conference after another. I wonder when we will have a laborer conference. The harvest depends on laborers, not leaders. In view of the situation, Jesus said to His followers, this is what I want you to do. I want you to pray. This clear injunctive has been there for 2000 years. However, for the most part, it has been disregarded for the same number of years. Why is this? Could it be that those who read these words just simply do not believe prayer will affect the harvest? Personally, I cannot think of any other answer to this question. Or it may be that we do not view prayer as labor. If you have such a view, consider Paul's letter to the Colossians. *"Epaphras, who is one of you, a bondservant of Christ, greets you, always laboring fervently for you in prayers, that you may stand perfect and complete in all the will of God"* (Colossians 4:12).

The harvest requires prayer laborers, but no one seems to be looking for this kind of position in the kingdom.

Jesus goes a little further. He says I not only want you to pray, but this is also how I want you to pray, and this is the one to whom I want you to pray. *"Pray, the Lord of the harvest"* (Matthew 9:38). Who is the Lord of the harvest? That can be no one other than Jesus. Jesus is Lord of the harvest. It is His harvest. He created and redeemed it. It is His in both the creative and redemptive sense. No part of it belongs to the Devil. Satan has no legal claim to any of it. The harvest belongs to God. So Jesus is saying I want you to ask me this: *"Ask me to send workers into my harvest"* (Matthew 9:38).

Remember Jesus was speaking to His disciples, not just the Twelve. These were the only potential workers He could send. So if Jesus was speaking then as He would today, He would have said. "I want you to ask me to send you into my harvest." Many have prayed, at some time, "Lord, send somebody." Few have prayed, "Lord, send me." The harvest depends on laborers; this I understand, but Lord, don't send me. We are afraid to pray "Lord, send me into Your harvest" because we are almost certain He would do it. Right? All kinds of pictures run through our minds when we think about these things because of the way the church has viewed this portion of Scripture.

Here is the way it goes. If I pray this prayer and the Lord answers, I will have to quit my job, give up my profession, go to seminary, get a degree in theology, be ordained by a local church or a denomination, and become a professional clergyman. This is not what Jesus had in mind. Though some may receive such a call, most will not. Jesus was talking to ordinary people. He was not suggesting they become professional preachers. He wanted them to get involved in the harvest of souls. He was calling laborers, not professionals. He wants those who desire to work.

Perhaps you are saying, "If these are His followers, why doesn't He just send them. Why do they need to ask?" In my mind, this has to do with free will. God does not force any one into the harvest. He waits for us to ask.

Let's take this one step further. Let's suppose you pray, "Lord, send me into Your harvest." Where do you think He would send you? To some foreign country? Some distant city? Probably not. Based on His Word, I believe He would send you to your own neighborhood. I say this because Jesus said, *"Love your neighbor"* (Mark 12:31), which is not a suggestion but a command. *"Love God, with all your heart, soul, mind, and strength and love your neighbor as yourself"* (Mark 12:30). Do you know your name? Do you know what you look like?

In spite of this clear word in Mark 12:31, we do not love our neighbors; we don't even know their names. George Barna of the Research Institute headquartered in California found through his research that 74% of Americans, Christian and non-Christian, do not know the names of their closest neighbors. That doesn't sound as if we love our neighbors.

I have observed over a lifetime of ministry that few Christians who have been in the church more than two years ever lead anyone to Christ or His church. In spite of all the training on soul-winning, they do not do it, and I believe there is a reason for this. New converts have friends in the world in whose lives they have a degree of influence. Some of those friends follow them to church and find the Lord. After a short time, they bring in those whose lives they have influenced to the church. Some become active in the ministry of the church and soon, their relationships with the unchurched die. Having little or no influence on the lives of those outside the church, they can no longer lead anyone to Christ.

In another report, Barna found that one out of four unchurched people in America say they would attend church if a friend invited them. If this report is accurate, we need to develop friendships with our unchurched neighbors. We should pray to build relationships with those who do not know the Lord in view of influencing their lives as Christians. When trouble comes, they will know who to call for help.

Too many Christians cannot see clearly. We are like the blind man who was brought to Jesus to be healed. Jesus touched him and asked, *"What do you see?"* He said, *"I see men they look like walking trees"* (Mark 8:24). Oh, yes, he could see; he was no longer blind, but for all practical purposes, he may as well have been. He saw people, but they looked like trees. There are many who have had a touch from the Lord, and they can see.

However, the question is not, can you see, it is what do you see?

The man's reply revealed a need to be touched again. Hence, Jesus touched him again and asked the same question. Then the man who had been blind, the man who had been touched and could see a little, could now see every man clearly. We need a second touch from God to see people clearly as Jesus does and be moved with compassion as He is when He sees people in their true conditions.

Several years ago, I opened the morning session of a great prayer conference in Los Angeles, CA with the following words: "Any program of the church that does not have as its primary focus and ultimate goal the salvation of the lost should be changed or scrapped." I have not changed my opinion. At times, churches swamp their people with all kinds of good things, but souls are not the primary focus. It may promote fellowship, connecting, feeding, fun or one of a hundred good things but not the salvation of the lost. *"Christ Jesus came into the world to save sinners"* (1 Timothy 1:15). This was the primary purpose of His mission. His part was accomplished when he sat down at the right hand of the throne of God in heaven. Our part is being accomplished at a snail's pace because it is not the major focus of ministry in today's church. Jesus said to His disciples, *"Go into all the world and share thee good news with every person. I will go with you. In my name you will cast out devils, you will take up serpents, you will speak with new tongues, if you drink any deadly thing it will not hurt you, you will lay hands on the sick and they will recover"* (Mark 16:15).

All of these promises are given in the context of evangelism. Signs will accompany anyone who responds to His call to go.

At first, Jesus sent out seventy-two. He gave them the power to heal the sick and cast out devils. They returned to Jesus rejoicing that demons were subject to them. His response to them was, *"You are rejoicing over the wrong thing. Rejoice, that your names are written in heaven"* (Luke 10:20). This is what really matters, but this is not to be the primary focus of the church. We are still majoring in minors. Programs by the score are implemented. Only one or two of them focus on the lost; most don't. Even our prayer meetings are not focused on the salvation of those who are lost. This is so in spite of the fact that most Christians know we were saved because someone prayed for us.

As you can see, I cannot stay off this subject. We have to align our wills with His. Our mission must be in absolute agreement with His. Then and only then can we see the work He began, completed.

PRAYER

Lord Jesus, touch us again. We see, but our vision is blurred. We see people as trees. We see the masses but cannot focus on individuals. We need to see better if we are to go and that is what we want to do.

Father, send me into Your harvest. Send me to my neighborhood. Send me to those with whom I work. Send me to the lost. Lead me to divine encounters. I want to help someone find You, to come to know You as Savior and Lord. Amen!

CHAPTER SEVEN

Prayer and the Will of God

Another question often asked by sincere Christians is how can I know the will of God? Some seem almost paranoid about possibly missing God's will. I've heard people say, "I think God is trying to tell me something." My response to that statement is: "God is not trying to do anything. If He wants to tell you something, He will." We are inclined to think of God in human terms, as if He were a man—only bigger and more powerful. Not so, *"As the heavens are higher than the earth, so are My ways higher than your ways, and My thoughts than your thoughts"* (Isaiah 55:9).

It is important to know His will, though it is not absolutely essential. However, I believe we can pray most effectively when we know just exactly what God's will is in a matter. Paul admonished the church at

Ephesus, *"Do not be unwise, but understand what the will of the Lord is"* (Ephesians 5:17).

In 1 John 5:14, 15 we read: *"This is the confidence that we have in Him, that if we ask anything according to His will, He hears us. And if we know that He hears us…we know that we have the petitions that we have asked of Him."* The qualifying phrase here is *"according to His will."* The promise is that we will receive an answer to our petitions. If we know His will, we can pray with greater faith. But you may ask, "How can I be sure that I know His will?"

REVELATION

One way to know God's will is by direct revelation. That is, He may speak a *rhema* word to us—anyone of us, mature or immature, educated or uneducated. Peter received such a word. Matthew 16:13-17 records that Jesus asked His disciples, *"Who do men say that I, the Son of Man, am?"* Their reply was, *"Some say John the Baptist, some Elijah, others Jeremiah or one of the prophets."* Then Jesus asked, *"But who do you say that I am?"* Immediately Peter answered, *"You are the Christ, the Son of the Living God."*

I think Peter surprised himself. He was not sure how he knew it but out came those words: *"You are the Christ."* Jesus responded, *"Blessed are you Simon son of*

Jonah, flesh and blood has not revealed this to you, but My Father who is in heaven" (Matthew 16:17). In effect, Jesus was saying, "Peter, you have received a revelation. It came from God and was not based on logic or reason." Peter could not have explained how he knew who Jesus was, but he did. Many of us have had such an experience. We know, but we don't know how we know. By an inner witness, we know and can say, *"You are the Christ."*

There are times when God speaks in such clear tones we think our ears heard something. Though I have never to my knowledge heard the audible voice of God, I have heard Him speak in my spirit many times. He speaks through inner impressions. He speaks through circumstances. He speaks through others. He speaks through His Word. When He is speaking to you, you will know it. His sheep know His voice. There is no doubt about it.

I have heard testimonies of people who, while living deep in sin, heard the voice of God so clearly they knew who it was. A dear friend of mine, who was formerly an atheist, once told me that while she was far away from God, He told her He loved her just as she was. She was so overwhelmed by His voice she followed Him from that very day and is now an evangelist.

God does not lead His people today by a pillar of fire and a cloud. He has given us His Spirit to live within us and to guide us in the ways He would have us go. You may not see or hear anything, but you can know God has spoken. In your "knower," that is, in your deepest being, you intuitively know God has spoken, and you perceive His will in a matter. When this happens, you may say, "I do not know how I know, but I do know God wants me to do this—or not do that."

There is a level of spiritual maturity where you know God's will because you have been walking so closely to His presence. You have heard His voice so often you know what to do when the time comes, even if you do not hear anything at the moment.

I was praying with a group of young men one morning in Texarkana, Arkansas. I had been shopping for a set of tires for the truck I used to pull our travel trailer. I had been looking and comparing but had not bought, though I had the money to do so. While praying that morning, I clearly heard the Lord say; "I want you to ask me for those tires." I knew that voice, and I also knew He had a purpose for saying those words to me.

I had been ministering about prayer in the church where I was praying with those young guys, and I knew

God wanted to demonstrate a truth I had been sharing. *"Seek first, the kingdom of God and His righteousness and all of the things you need will be added to you"* (Matthew 6:33). I had taught, keep your priorities in proper order and the Lord will take care of all your needs. When He authorizes you to ask, you can be sure God is going to work in a supernatural way.

When we had finished, I shared with these friends what the Lord had told me. I explained that they were not to try to buy me a set of tires. The tires would come from a source that knew nothing about what I had shared with them. The next day, I returned to our home, which at that time was in Northwest Arkansas. The very next day, one of our spiritual sons came by with his company's check book, the big one. Before he left, he gave me a check for National Call to Prayer for $200.00 as he had often done before. He mentioned nothing about tires, so I knew this was not my answer.

The next day, the same person called and said, "If you have time, I'd like you to come by my office. I want to take you to my tire shop. I want to buy you a set of tires for your truck." When I got to his office a day or two later, I said to him, "Ben, I want to know why you said you wanted to buy me a set of tires for my truck?" His response was, "I thought that is what God said to me." I told him the rest of the story so he would know that God had indeed spoken to him, and it was good he had obeyed. Then he said, "I need to tell you the rest of my story." He said, "When I came by your house on Sunday I left you a check for $200.00 and as I was driving away from your house, the Lord said to me, 'Ben, I told you to leave a check for $300.00, now because you did not obey me, I am requiring you to buy him a set of tires for his truck." We had a good laugh. Remembering that story, I often remind people that it may cost less to obey the first time; it might cost more if we don't.

Some people might call such a thing a "holy hunch." I call it "knowing in your spirit." In his book *The Spiritual Man*, Watchman Nee says that one of the functions of the human spirit is to "know things intuitively." When the human spirit is alive and filled with the Spirit of God, it functions the way it was designed to. And when the human spirit is functioning the way it was designed to, it will hear the voice of God. It will know the will of the Father.

Jesus' spirit functioned properly. He always knew the will of the Father. "But," I hear someone object, "He is the Son of God. He had inside information." It is true; He is the Son of God. But we who have been born from above are also, *"children of God"* (1 John 3:2). And we have a reborn spirit that has the potential to hear God and to know the will of our Father: *"As many as are led by the Spirit of God, these are the sons of God"* (Romans 8:14).

We have the same access to the Father that Jesus had as a man. Jesus was living as any other human being while He was here on the earth. To know the will of His Father, He had to spend quality time with Him. The same is true of us.

This leads me to the second way we come to know His will: through relationship. To know God's will truly, we need to know Him. When we really know Him, we know His will. This is what I have referred to earlier in this book. Work on your relationship with God. Get to know Him.

Knowing God is the highest pursuit in which a human can be involved. The apostle Paul had experienced great hardship in his pursuit of knowing God; yet, in his letter to the Philippians, he still expressed this as the deepest desire of his heart: *"That I may know Him and the power of His resurrection, and the fellowship of His sufferings"* (Philippians 3:10). Paul was saying, *"I want to know Him as intimately and completely as I know He can be known."* Then in Colossians 1:9, Paul said he prays diligently for other Christians to be *"filled with the knowledge of His will in all wisdom and spiritual understanding."* My desire for you is that you may get to know Christ—to know Him as intimately as I know He can be known. When you know Him, you will know His will. And when you know Him and His will, you will align your will with His will and pray on the earth what God wills in heaven.

How do we get to know Him? We get to know God exactly as we would get to know anyone. We must spend quality time with Him—in conversation. If you can do that over a period of years, you will know His nature and character. And when you know His nature and His character, you will be able to look at a given situation and know His will. You will know that He never acts contrary to His nature or out of character.

Listen to people talk about the things of God, and you will discern very quickly what they know of His nature and character. Listen to them read the Bible, and you can hear by the tone they give to the voice of God just how well they know Him.

For many years now, I have read the Bible with no other purpose in mind than to know God as He is revealed in His Holy Word. I have long since given up trying to prop up my doctrines with Scripture verses scattered here and there. A long time ago, I found that you could prove just about anything with the Word of God if you are subtle enough. My understanding of God and my knowledge of Him have come from spending quality time in His presence, listening to what He says. I do not come into His presence to have Him agree with me. I come to agree with Him. He is always right. And as I meditate on His Word, I begin to know His nature and His character. His Word tells me what He has done, what He is going to do, and how He has dealt with different situations in the lives of His people. As I learn, I am corrected and encouraged. I am changed into His image. Hallelujah!

I do not read His Word to find out when Jesus is coming back. I am discovering, through His truth, that He is already here. Jesus could not be more real if He were to manifest Himself in the flesh. How can I say such a thing? Well, Paul says *we don't know Christ according to the flesh* (2 Corinthians 5:16)—*we know our Lord through the Spirit.* If He were here in His physical body, He would be confined to a specific place. However, as He is now, I can live across the world from Him and never see Him. But through the indwelling Spirit I can have a continuous, living relationship with my Lord. He is as real as life itself.

Jesus said to His disciples, *"It is to your advantage that I go away"* (John 16:7). I believe what He said. Yes, I believe He is returning to this earth in bodily form—and this refers to the body He left in, not the church. In Acts 1:11, right after our Lord's ascension, an angel told the disciples, *"This same Jesus…will so come in like manner as you saw Him go into heaven."*

WHAT IS GOD LIKE?

Let's take a closer look at who God is. Here is what the apostle John has to say, *"Beloved, let us love one another, for love is of God; and everyone who loves is born of God and knows God. He who does not love does not know God, for 'God is love"* (1 John 4:7, 8).

In His true essence, the unchanging God is love. Therefore, He is compassionate, merciful, patient, forgiving—not willing that even one should perish. He does not have to try to be merciful. To be unmerciful is contrary to His nature. It is not an effort for Him to be patient. Because He is love, He is patient. God is not patient just on the days He feels good. He does not forgive because He is in a forgiving mood. It is His nature. He cannot be love and be unkind. Unforgiveness is contrary to His nature. Man's conduct cannot change the nature of God. He does not change. We have His word on the matter.

The English word "love" is used often in the New Testament in reference to God. In the Greek the noun is *agape* and the verb *agapeo*. *Agape* is who God is. *Agapeo* is what He does to show us who He is. Unlike us, God loves the unlovely. He loved us when we were sinners, when we were living in willful disobedience and rebellion: *"But God demonstrates His own love toward us, in that while we were still sinners, Christ died for us"* (Romans 5:8). His love is not limited to a few select ones: *"For God so loved the world that He gave His only begotten Son, that whoever believes in Him should not perish but have everlasting life"* (John 3:16).

What is the "good news" of the gospel? It can be stated in a few words: *"God is love"* (1 John 4:7). Until Jesus came, the world had little understanding of what God was really like. God had revealed His holy character but only a few were aware of His loving nature. The Old Testament reveals His character. The New Testament reveals His nature. His nature is love; His character is holy. This distinction is very important.

In the Word, God is called the Holy One or the Holy One of Israel forty-seven times. In the book of Revelation, one of the seven angels declares, *"You are righteous, O Lord"* (Revelation 16:5). God Himself said, *"I the Lord your God am holy"* (Leviticus 19:2). These words, "holy" and "righteous" are adjectives used to describe an attribute of God. God who is love in His true essence and nature is holy in character. His holy character requires Him to do right. Not what you or I think is right, but what *is* right. God always knows and does right. Like Paul, I do not know Him as well as I want to. That is why I set aside time daily to be in His presence. If others seem to know Him better than you do, it may be that they are spending more time with Him.

Jesus always knew His father's will because He spent time alone with Him in the place of prayer. That is why He could say:

"The Son can do nothing of Himself, but (only) what He sees the Father do" (John 5:19).

"I do not seek my own will but the will of the Father who sent me" (John 5:30).

"The words that I speak to you I do not speak on My own authority; but the Father who dwells in Me does the works" (John 14:10).

Jesus was totally submissive to the Father; He had no will of His own. Isn't that where we want to be in our spiritual walk?

JESUS KNEW HIS FATHER'S WILL, SO CAN YOU

It is clear that Jesus did the Father's will, but how could He always be sure of what His Father willed? The answer can be seen in the record of His walk on the earth. Mark reports, *"Having risen a long while before daylight, He went out and departed to a solitary place; and there He prayed"* (Mark 1:35). Matthew tells us that after Jesus left the multitude, *"He went up on a mountain by Himself to pray"* (Matthew 14:23). He was always going to or coming from the place of prayer. At times He spent all night praying.

Jesus was so in tune with His Father that He could say, "When I heal someone, I am doing exactly what My Father has told Me to do. When I raise someone from the dead, I am doing exactly what My Father has told Me to do. When I cast out demons, I am doing exactly what My Father has told Me to do.

Jesus did not even attempt to do anything unless His Father told Him to do it. Sometimes He healed every person in a place. Other times, He healed only one among a multitude. He stopped a few funeral processions in His lifetime and raised people to life again, but not all. He did just what His Father told Him to do—no more and no less. And remember, to His disciples He said, *"As the Father has sent Me, I also send you"* (John 20:21). It is evident from these words that we are in the world, not to do our will but the will of Him who sent us.

If we are in this world to do His will, it is best that we know what it is. How will we know His will if we do not spend quality time in His presence? And how will we hear His voice if we do all the talking? We must be listeners when we come into His presence.

Knowing the will of God is simple but not easy. It is simple because it requires nothing more than spending quality time in the presence of the One whose will you seek to know. That's all. But that is not easy because of the demands of the flesh. The flesh wants to "do" something—go into action. To the flesh, prayer is a passive endeavor. But the truth of the matter is that nothing we do will make any real difference unless the Holy Spirit motivates it. For a work to be a work of God it must be conceived through the Spirit in the place of prayer and be carried out in the energy of the Spirit.

Anything else, regardless of how it may appear, is a work of the flesh. It may be a good work, but good works of the flesh are not acceptable to God. He does not see things as we do. Hence the Scriptures warn that many who are first here will be last in the presence of God. He knows which works are of Him and which are of the flesh. We may call some works good; He may call them bad. We may call some spiritual; He may call them carnal. Remember, His ways are higher than ours.

It seems the disciples followed the example the Lord set before them. Acts Chapter 1 says that after the Lord's ascension, about 120 of His followers went back into Jerusalem and continued in prayer.

Acts Chapter 2 records that as they prayed, the Holy Spirit was poured out upon them and they experienced miraculous manifestations of His presence. These manifestations were so unusual that a multitude of people—many from other nations—came together to see what was going on. Many foreigners were astonished when they heard these Galileans speaking their native languages; some thought they were drunk with wine. But as a result of Peter preaching Jesus, three thousand souls repented and received baptism. Then we read in Acts 2:42: *"They continued steadfastly in the apostles' doctrine and fellowship, in the breaking of bread, and in prayers."* Somehow, those new converts knew they were to pray. *"And as they prayed the Lord kept adding to the church daily those who were being saved"* (Acts 2:47).

In Acts Chapter 3, we see Peter and John going to the temple at the time of prayer. On their way to the prayer meeting, a paralytic beggar asked them for some money. Peter said, *"I don't have money, but I do have something you need more than money. In the name of Jesus Christ of Nazareth, rise up and walk."* The power of God went through that poor man and suddenly, he was running through the temple, walking, leaping, and praising God (Acts 3:1-10).

This story illustrates just how important it is to know the will of God. We can do only the things He has authorized. It is quite possible that Jesus Himself had passed by this beggar previously. Scripture says the man was past forty years of age, and he lay daily at the temple gate called Beautiful in Jerusalem. Jesus entered Jerusalem through that gate and had not ministered to this man. Why? Jesus did only what His Father told Him to do. As said before. At times Jesus healed everyone present in a place; other times, He healed only a few.

For some time, Peter and John had been going up to the temple to pray day after day; yet, they did not minister to this man. But on this day, Peter had the authority to do what he did. Obviously, the Lord had spoken to him. There is no reason to believe Peter had greater faith that day than the day before. There is also no evidence to sustain the view that the beggar had greater faith that day. Peter did not have a sudden burst of internal energy, which made it possible for him to minister successfully to this poor man. So what was different about that day? I believe it was that at that very moment, Peter received specific authority to minister healing to this man. Peter was so in tune with God that he knew what to do.

Is such a relationship possible now? Yes! It is possible, but it is not easy because of the weakness of the flesh. However, if we do not believe that such a relationship is possible, we will never try to enter it. James says, *"Draw near to God and He will draw near to you"* (James 4:8). Moses put it another way: *"You will find Him is you seek Him with all your heart and with all your soul"* (Deuteronomy 4:29).

Diligence is required. The whole heart and soul must seek God. And the seeking must be directed toward His face, and not His hand. Far too many of us are so interested in His hand and what we hope to receive from it that we never seek His face. If you want to see His hand, seek His face. Seek His hand only, and you will see neither His hand nor His face.

Paul was not seeking anything from God; he simply wanted to know Him. That would be enough. Anything God would do for Paul was insignificant compared to knowing Him. And Paul knew that knowing God would require more than giving Him a few minutes when he could fit it into his busy schedule. Knowing God was a priority. If we are to know Him, we must be prepared to give Him the best time of our day.

I've read that John Wesley's mother spent two hours each day in communication with her Lord—in spite of the fact that she had fifteen children to care for. She wanted to know Him, and she knew it would take time, quality time, in His presence.

After more than sixty years in the school of prayer, I believe I can speak from the wisdom of experience. Early morning is the time for prayer. Jesus arose long before daylight and went to prayer (Mark 1:35). I have found that if I do not begin the day with prayer, I often end it the way it began. The mind is fresh in the morning; the body is renewed and rested. The first hour is the best hour, and I have determined to give my best to God. David says in Psalm 5:3: *"My voice you shall hear in the morning, O Lord; in the morning I will direct (my prayer) to You, and I will look up."*

You may be saying, *"I just can't get up in the morning; I'm a night person."* My question to you is: *"Are you a house of prayer?"* If you are, no problem; continue the way you are. Whether you have established time in the morning or at night, keep your schedule with God.

In the early church, there were set hours of prayer. Acts 3:1 tells us that one of those hours was 3:00 p.m. Some believe that early Christians followed the patterns of the Jews in prayer: they prayed at 6:00 a.m., 3:00 p.m., and 9:00 p.m. From the evidence presented in the book of Acts, they prayed at other times as well. If you read Acts Chapter 3 carefully, you will see that the early church had a set time and an established place for daily prayer.

Study the lives of the Old Testament saints. They spent much time seeking God. In fact, David said, *"As the deer pants for the water brooks, so pants my soul for You, O God. My soul thirsts for God, for the living God"* (Psalm 42:1, 2). Isaiah cried out, *"With my soul I have desired You in the night; yes, by my spirit within me I will seek You early"* (Isaiah 26:9).

When we seek God with that kind of diligence, we will know Him and His will. When we know His will, we can pray intelligently about matters. When we pray intelligently about a matter, there will be an answer every time. When we enter this dimension, we no longer pray and hope; we pray and expect the answer to come. Some may say that it is not possible to enter this kind of relationship with God, and we cannot always hope to know the will of God. My response is Jesus did. Jesus always knew His Father's will and if He did, we can. We *can* spend the time necessary to know God. But the question is will we? Will we take the time required to know God?

PRAYER

Father, my desire is to know You. When I know You I will know Your will. Draw me nearer. I need and want to be close to You. I want to live with an awareness of Your presence, not just occasionally but every moment of every day. Amen!

Chapter Eight

Effective Prayer

James wrote in his epistle: *"The effectual fervent prayer of a righteous man, availeth much"* (James 5:16). I thought it necessary to expand that verse a little bit: "The fervent heart-felt prayer of a person in right standing with God through faith in Jesus Christ, evidenced by humility and an obedient regard for His will, as revealed in His word, is powerful and effective." A prayer may be fervent but not effective. However, I am not sure it can be effective but not fervent, at least, not on a consistent basis. I have seen in my lifetime many people praying very fervently about situations in their lives but without results. This happens when prayer is not accompanied by faith, humility, and obedience. Pain or trouble may have brought a display of fervency, but that is not enough. Islamic people pray persistently, but persistence is not enough.

The very use of the word, effectual, implies that some prayers may be ineffectual. Any one who has ever prayed has probably prayed a few ineffectual prayers. I am sure I have, but I am learning to pray effectually and I want to share some of these truths with you.

To be effective, prayer must be accompanied with true humility. On this matter, James says: *"God resists the proud, but blesses the humble in spirit"* (James 4:6). We all have a lot of pride in us—in some more than others—but enough to block our prayers. Humility is not an act. To act as if you are humble when, in fact, you are not is only a display of false humility. Pure and true humility has to do with your view of God. The closer we come to Him, the smaller we become in our own eyes. The less adequate we feel in our own strength. Prayer is human weakness calling on God's strength. It is human ignorance calling on divine wisdom. It is mortal inability calling on immortal ability. For some, all options have to be gone before they can call for help. But God spoke to Solomon and said: *"If my people who are called by my name will humble themselves and pray...I will hear"* (2 Chronicles 7:14). Anything less than true humility will delay the answer and may cancel it altogether.

A study of the nation of Israel, God's chosen ones, reveals a cycle they have experienced over and over throughout their history. God makes a covenant with them. They agree to the terms of the covenant, walk in God's blessings for a while and then take His blessings for granted. Pride fills the hearts of leaders and people; they trust in their own accomplishments. God sends His prophet to warn them. They respond by stoning the prophet or disregarding him. As a result, God's judgment falls upon them. They repent and cry out to Him for mercy. Humility is now their attitude.

God raises up a godly leader who leads them back into fellowship. God's Word is again held in high regard. Revival comes and blessings return but then the cycle begins all over again. What a pity. You might think man would eventually learn; however, it seems he continues to trust in himself and walk in pride. It's as if he created himself by his own will and sustains himself through his own efforts. God, have mercy on us.

For prayer to be effective, humility must be followed by obedience to the will of God as revealed in His Word. The more I think about it, the more I am convinced that obedience always follows and never precedes humility. It is the truly humble who consistently obey, and those who obey, pray. It is the humble people who are not hesitant to show emotions when they pray. They will cry aloud with tears. It doesn't matter who sees. They want to be heard and are not afraid to show it. Tears often accompany heart-felt prayers. Loud cries are often heard when people are desperate. My dear, humble little mother often prayed with tears. In fact, she could hardly say the name of Jesus without tears welling up in her eyes. Lord, keep us humble and praying with tears of deep concern.

I am not saying that to be effective in prayer you must pray with tears. However, it seems from a study of the Word that our Father has high regard for the prayers of those who humbly pray and shed tears of deep concern. The perceived gravity of a given situation will determine how we approach it. If I am emotionally involved with the person or situation about which I am praying, those emotions will bleed through. Tears and loud cries may be seen and heard. Hebrews 7:5 tells us that Jesus, while He was here on the earth *"lifted up his voice with strong crying and tears unto God."* At times, Jesus got emotional when he prayed. Being truly humble, he showed his emotions when the situation stirred them up. An honest show of emotions is always in order when we pray.

Solomon, the wisest King who ever led the nation of Israel knew the human tendency to grow cold and forget the blessings of God. A picture of this is seen in 2 Chronicles Chapter 6 and 7. The temple had just been dedicated and the presence of God had manifested in a most unusual way. Being wise, Solomon knew these feelings of devotion to God would wane. As a result, he prayed to God for his people about a matter before it actually happened. It goes something like this:

"Father, I know it is possible Your people will turn away from You and You may have to send judgment to get their attention. I pray, that if and when this happens, if they turn their faces to this temple that I have built and dedicated to You, hear them and answer their prayers."

Then God answers in 2 Chronicles 7:13, 14, *"If I shut the heavens that there be no rain, and if I send pestilence among the people and locust to devour the land, If my people who are called by my name will humble themselves and pray and seek my face, I will hear from heaven, forgive their sins and heal their land."*

The key here is humility. Before prayer, humility must come. There can be no effectual prayer apart from true humility. What about volume? Again, the perceived gravity of the situation will determine the volume with which we approach it. If while driving down your street early in the morning you happen to see smoke pouring from underneath the eaves of a house with the lights out, assuming people were asleep in the house, you wouldn't knock gently on the door. No! You would make as much noise as possible. Lives may be in danger. People could die. You might not even know who lives there, but you would not drive by with indifference.

Prayer can be approached in the same manner. When we are moved by the fact that unsaved people are in a burning house, we cannot, we must not drive by. What I have said does not adequately depict the enormity of the situation. It is not just the loss of temporal life that makes the matter so serious, but the possibility of losing eternal life in the presence of the Father.

Effective prayer must be accompanied by faith. We must believe that we receive the thing for which we ask. This is where many feel weak and are not sure they have sufficient faith to pray effectively. We know some amount of faith is required, but we don't know how much. Unfortunately, many believe that whatever the amount, it is more than they have.

A careful reading of Scripture reveals that though all of us who believe receive a measure of faith, we do not all have the same amount. We may have started our walk with the Lord with the seed of faith He planted in our hearts, but faith has the potential to grow, mature, and produce fruit in believers. Your faith is growing at some rate. Perhaps you are saying, "I believe my faith is dormant. It seems I have less than when I first believed." Jesus identified this state of faith by referring to some as having little faith and others weak in faith. Some are recognized as having great faith while others have no faith at all.

Can anything be done to grow your faith from weak to strong or little to much? This is a question that needs to be answered. I am glad to report that your faith can grow and become stronger and stronger, but you may not know when it is strong. Why is this? It is because faith is a gift from God to those who pray. *"Lord, increase our faith"* is what the apostles prayed. Like revelation, faith is an outgrowth of a relationship with God. Faith comes by hearing a word from God (Romans 10:17).

I remember complaining to God on one occasion about not being able to hear His voice. His response to my complaint was "Son, you should know that hearing has to do with proximity." In others words, move a little closer. In the words of James *"Draw near to God and He will draw near to you"* (James 4:8).

God wants a close relationship with His children, but He waits for us to initiate it. He wants us to draw near. A close relationship with God begins with desire, which is expressed through sincere prayer. God draws near to those who draw near to Him. In this experience of nearness, a relationship is built, and faith is strengthened.

Multitudes of believers are acquainted with God but do not know Him. Consequently, their trust levels are very low. You cannot trust a person you do not know. The better you know God the more fully you will trust Him.

Believe it or not, you have faith in some amount. The seed is planted in the soil of your soul. It has the potential to grow. How fast, deep, and strong it becomes will depend, to a great deal, on how well you nurture it. Exercise your faith in areas known to be the will of God. Pray His will, and you will always have His answer.

Jesus was always successful in prayer because His requests were not motivated by the need that seemed to exist. He prayed according to His Father's will. He did only what His Father told Him to do. Worthy of repeating is the fact that at times, Jesus healed everyone in a given place. Yet, other times, he healed only one or a few at most. As mentioned earlier, it is reasonable to believe he passed the paralytic who begged daily at the Beautiful Gate of the temple. Jesus, Peter, and John had passed him at that very gate on numerous occasions. But on the appointed day when Peter was confronted with a request for alms he said, *"Silver and gold have I none, but such as I have I give you. In the Name of Jesus Christ of Nazareth, rise and walk"* (Acts 3:6).

He did as he was told having been healed by the mighty power of a word spoken through a mortal by the Holy Spirit. That day, Peter had the authority to perform this miracle. At the time, Jesus passed through that same gate, He was not authorized to meet the beggar's real need.

It all has to do with hearing what the Lord is saying. Live your life everyday with an awareness of His presence. Keep your eyes and ears open and God will work His will through your life. No, you don't need a big name. You do not have to be a preacher, evangelist, or missionary. The ability to do the works of Jesus will come to those who are available and not afraid to act on His behalf when the Spirit moves. Much more would be accomplished if more of us would spend enough time in God's presence to get familiar with His voice. All of His sheep recognize His voice, but many do not understand what He is saying.

PRAYER

Father, open our ears; anoint them with ear salve. We are so dull of hearing. The noise of the world has deafened us. May we quiet ourselves in Your presence and listen for Your Word. The presence of a need does not necessarily indicate we are called to meet it. We must do only what You tell us to do—nothing less and nothing more. We can do nothing without you and with you, all things are possible.

Father, increase our faith. Teach us to use the little faith we have until it becomes strong, and we become strong in the Lord and in Your strength. We want to pray prayers You will be pleased to answer. Amen!

Chapter Nine

Because You Did Not Ask

Jesus spent quite a lot of time teaching His disciples by word and example about the importance of prayer. On one occasion, He said to them, *"Seek first, the kingdom of God and His righteousness, and all of these things will be added unto you"* (Matthew 6:33). Just before He gave this word, He had assured them their Father knew what they needed before they asked Him. It seems that our Lord was trying to help us, His disciples, to understand that our needs are seen by a loving Father who has committed the resources of heaven toward meeting them.

Many are living today who may have had irresponsible fathers. Nevertheless, once you become a child of God, you can rest assured Your heavenly Father knows exactly what you need. He has promised to meet all our needs according to His riches in glory. Our heavenly Father is a responsible Father. He chose and adopted each of us. He made us a part of His family. In so doing, He became responsible for our welfare: physical, spiritual, material, and emotional. Our God will not fail to keep His word on our behalf. However, some of the things we do bring us His special attention.

In 1 Kings Chapter 3, we find recorded the history of Solomon's (David's son) coronation. David, who was now a very old man, had chosen Solomon to be his successor as the King of Israel. Solomon was still quite young and inexperienced and his first action as king was to carry out the instructions his father David had given regarding some people who had made trouble for him while he served Israel as king. Having completed this task, he called all the people, from the least to the greatest, together at Gibeon. There, he offered a thousand burnt offerings to the Lord. In 1 Kings 3:5, God says to Solomon, *"Ask for whatever you want me to give you."* Immediately, Solomon replied, *"Give me wisdom and knowledge, that I may lead this people, for who is able to govern this great people of yours."*

The record states that God was pleased with this request and responded. *"Since this is your heart's desire, and because you did not ask for wealth, riches and honor, nor the death of your enemies, and since you did not ask me for long life, but for wisdom and knowledge, therefore wisdom and knowledge will be given you and I will give you (what you did not ask for) wealth, riches, honor such as no king before you, nor, none after you has or will ever possess"* (2 Corinthians 1:11). What a promise. God was extremely pleased with Solomon's request.

If God said to you, ask for whatever you want me to give you, what would be your request? Think about it. What is truly in your heart will be revealed by your response. Many of us would probably ask for physical health or healing for our bodies. Others would ask for material wealth, marital bliss or other blessings that affect the emotions. Others would ask for spiritual things or pray, "Father, I only want the wisdom and knowledge to successfully do what You have commissioned me to do. I want to fulfill my mission in life."

Jesus put it this way: Pray *"Thy kingdom come, thy will be done in earth as it is in heaven"* (Matthew 6:10). What is your list of priorities? Do you have one? Have you listed first things in first place? How do you begin your day? Do you rise up in the morning and pray: "May Your lordship be established and Your will done in my life and in my family today"? Are you concerned about your church family? Do you pray for members of the household of faith? This is a prayer the Lord Jesus is sure to answer. Furthermore, it is a prayer with which

He is well pleased. However, this is not a formula for getting God to do your secret will.

We cannot "con" God, He knows our hearts and secret desires. He is not impressed with pleasant words, even those that seem right. God is looking for sincerity. The One who sees and knows also has the power to change. He once said to Israel, *"I will give you a new heart and a new spirit"* (Ezekiel 36:26). But that promise is not only to Israel. He will do this for anyone.

Do you need a new heart, spirit, and desires? Ask and you will receive is the promise of our Lord. Ask and keep on asking. Knock and keep on knocking; the door will open. *"It is the Father's good pleasure to give you the kingdom"* (Luke 12:32). By the Spirit, Paul says we should not be weary and lose heart in well doing because in due season we will reap, so don't give up (Galatians 6:9). Sometimes we receive things without asking. However, other times, answers only come because of our persistence.

PERSISTENT PRAYER

If there is one thing clearly taught by the Master, it is that receiving answers to prayer is often the result of persistence in prayer. Jesus shows us that simple, persistent prayer is, in fact, the evidence of great faith.

Consider the story of the Canaanite woman recorded in Matthew 15:21-28:

> [21]*Then Jesus went out from there and departed to the region of Tyre and Sidon.* [22]*And behold, a woman of Canaan came from that region and cried out to Him, saying, "Have mercy on me, O Lord, Son of David! My daughter is severely demon-possessed."*

> [23]*But He answered her not a word.*

> *And His disciples came and urged Him, saying, "Send her away, for she cries out after us."*

> [24]*But He answered and said, "I was not sent but to the lost sheep of the tribe of Israel.*[25]*Then she came and worshiped Him, saying, "Lord, help me!"*

> [26]*But He answered and said, "It is not right to take bread and throw it to the dogs."*

> [27]*And she said, "Yes, Lord, yet even the little dogs eat the crumbs which fall from their masters' table."*

> [28]*Then Jesus answered and said to her, "O woman great is your faith, be it unto you as you desire." And her daughter was healed from that very hour.*

Here is a woman who pressed her case until she received an appropriate response. At first, he answered her <u>not a word</u>. Have you ever been there? I have. I cried unto the Lord from the bottom of my heart, but there was no answer—not a word. Not yes, no, maybe, wait awhile—nothing but silence—only silence from the One who had the power to change the situation.

This was the awful experience of this desperate woman. Her daughter was in need, and she knew Jesus could help. She knew He could cast out demons. He had the power to meet her need. If that were not enough, she could hear His disciples, probably the Twelve saying, "Send her away!" She is bothering us with her cries. Jesus' answer implies they might have said: *"Lord, answer her or send her away, her cries are disturbing the meeting."*

Interestingly, those who had walked closest to the Lord had little sympathy for those who were in need. You will find such people in the church today. They do not know how to respond to those who come with needs so great they can't control their emotions. They cry for help but are ignored or asked to leave.

Neither the attitude of the Lord's disciples nor the Lord's response to their suggestion deterred this woman. Listen to what Jesus said to them in her hearing, *"I was sent only to the lost sheep of Israel."* Instead of leaving at this point, the woman came and knelt down before Him and said, *"Lord, help me."* Then, for the first time, Jesus spoke directly to her, *"It is not right to take the children's bread and toss it to their dogs."* His words were harsh and unlike any He had ever spoken to someone in need. What a biased, uncaring remark! You are a Gentile dog, and it would not be right (it would be wrong) for Me to do anything for you. Hear the persistence of this mother. *"Yes, Lord I am a dog, but even dogs have a right to the crumbs, which fall from their master's table"* (Matthew 15:27).

I am certain Jesus wanted His disciples and us to see how persistence in prayer prevails. Here, we see clearly that delay is not denial. His first answer is not always His final word in a matter. The woman was not asking the Lord to do anything other than what He had been doing. She would not stop until she received the answer her heart was set on. *"Great is your faith, your request is granted"* (Matthew 15:28). That's what she wanted to hear. Request granted. Now she could rejoice.

Dear reader, don't give up; press your claim. If your request doesn't violate the nature or character of God but would bring glory to His name, keep praying. The answer will come. Silence or delay is not necessarily a denial of your request. Persistence is evidence of great faith. As your faith is, so be it unto you. Read again the parable of the unjust judge found in Luke 18:1-8. Be encouraged to persist in prayer until the answer comes.

¹Then He spoke a parable to them, that men always ought to pray and not lose heart, ²saying: "There was in a certain city a judge who did not fear God nor regard man. ³Now there was a widow in that city; and she came to him, saying, 'Get justice for me from my adversary.' ⁴And he would not for a while; but afterward he said within himself, 'Though I do not fear God nor regard man, ⁵yet because this widow troubles me I will avenge her, lest by her continual coming she weary me.'"

⁶Then the Lord said, "<u>Hear what the unjust judge said.</u> ⁷And shall God not avenge His own elect who cry out day and night to Him, though He bears long with them? ⁸I tell you that He will avenge them speedily. Nevertheless, when the Son of Man comes, will He really find faith on the earth? (Luke 18:1-8)

Again, the Lord Jesus encourages us to persist in prayer. In this case, the word is, He will answer *quickly*. There is a time to patiently wait and a time to expect an answer to come quickly. Admittedly, some matters cannot wait, they require a speedy response. When you have lost control of the car, and it is skidding toward a deep gorge, you cannot wait for an answer. It has to come fast, and it will. A cry of desperation will often receive a quick response. When we pray for an unsaved loved one, we should expect a quick response. This prayer is in sync with the will of God who doesn't want anyone to be lost. He wants everyone to come to repentance. Years of experience in prayer has caused me to believe that the depth of intensity with which we pray often determines the speed with which a prayer is answered. And often, it is not the faith of the individual who is praying that produces results, even though faith is generally required.

Several years ago I read the testimony of Ken Gaub an evangelist who often traveled with his family to fulfill the call of God upon his life. Ken was traveling with his family in their motor home across the country on their way to Pennsylvania for a vacation. As they were driving along in the State of Ohio, he said to his wife, "Honey, I think God has lost my number. I don't seem to be able to hear him. He hasn't called me for awhile." Ken was depressed, and it showed. The kids saw a pizza parlor and as it was close to lunchtime asked their dad to stop. As the kids piled out of the bus, Ken made no attempt to leave his place at the steering wheel. His wife asked, "Are you not eating?"

To which Ken replied, "I'm not hungry. I'm just going over to that Dairy Queen and get a cold drink. I'll be here when you get back." That's what he did.

On his way back to the coach, he passed by a telephone booth in which the phone was ringing. No one being around, on an impulse, he picked up the phone and answered, "Hello."

The voice of the operator said, "Is this Reverend Gaub?"

In shock, he began to look for the hidden camera, thinking he might be on "Candid Camera."

Again the operator asked, "Is this Ken Gaub?"

To which he replied. "Yes, it is."

Another voice responded, "O, Reverend Gaub, I am so glad I got you. You see, this morning I was so depressed that I did not want to live. I thought if there was a God He sure didn't want to have anything to do with me. In this frame of mind, I sat down to write a note to the person who would find my body. My intention was to commit suicide.

"As I sat there with paper and a pencil in hand, I started to write when I suddenly remembered seeing you on television and wondered if you might be able to help me. As I was thinking in this vein, numbers began to come to my mind, and I wrote them on the paper. What I had written looked like a telephone number. I thought, could this possibly be the number of Reverend Gaub? It was at that point that I decided to make a person-to-person call because I thought if this is his number I will know there is a God and He cares about me. I called the operator and placed a person-to-person call not dreaming I would get your office."

Ken responded, "Lady, this is not my office; this is a telephone booth in Dayton, Ohio. I just happened to be passing by and on an impulse answered the phone which was ringing."

Apply the law of compound probability to that scenario. Of course, Ken ministered to a need God was already dealing with and in the process had his own need met. When his wife returned to the motor home, Ken said, *"Honey, you are not going to believe what just happened. God has not lost my number."*

A quick answer was needed. The situation was grave. A life was about to be lost. There was a cry for help and though not audible, it was heard. We serve a great God who knows and loves us. Even though the prayer was feeble and there was little, if any, faith, our God heard and answered. To me, this is one of the most revealing responses of a loving Father to a human need I ever heard. Ken's need and the need of this young lady were both met by God through the Holy Spirit.

PRAYER

Father, many people need a quick response. They cannot wait. Time is of essence. You are a loving God who has all power. Hear the cries of the desperate and answer quickly I pray. In the name of Jesus, our Lord. Amen.

CHAPTER TEN

Unrealistic Expectations

One of the most puzzling problems faced by many Bible-believing Christians is reconciling the seemingly limitless positive promises of the Word with the actual experience of activating them. We read the Scriptures, which we are told mean what they say. Hence, to the best of our ability, we obey them; yet, nothing happens.

"Call to Me, and I will answer you, and show you great and mighty things, which you do not know" (Jeremiah 33:3).

"Whatever things you ask when you pray, believe that you receive them, and you will have them" (Mark 11:24).

"If two of you agree on earth concerning anything that they ask, it will be done for them by My Father in heaven" (Matthew 18:19).

These promises seem to be unlimited. They appear to say anyone can ask anything, anytime, and it will be done. However, this does not appear to be the experience of many who pray. They ask very sincerely, firmly believing God can do what they ask, but nothing happens. Why doesn't God do what He said He would do? These promises seem to cover every need: physical, financial, spiritual, and emotional. But do they really? Are there qualifications and/or limitations that are not stated? Recognizing that I am treading on "holy ground," I will choose my words very deliberately. After many years of walking with the Lord, I am convinced that every promise of God has limitations, either stated or implied.

ARE GOD'S PROMISES LIMITED?

When we speak, we expect those who hear to understand the things we say at the present moment in the context of what we have said in the past. That is why we must read *all* of God's Word. All of God's promises have a relevant context; we cannot lift a promise out of its setting and stand on it. To do so can be very disappointing. On the surface, some promises seem to be unlimited. However, when you study them more carefully in view of the context in which they were given, they may, in fact, be limited. To understand them properly, you must examine them in the context of the entire revelation of God, His nature, His character, and His Word.

God will not do things for me that are contrary to His loving nature. Moreover, He will not do anything that will impugn His holy character. He will not do anything wrong. He does not answer the prayers of rebels and the willfully disobedient, unless those prayers are for forgiveness. He will not answer those who are selfish and self-centered. God will not do for us what He has given us the responsibility to do for ourselves. We cannot, through prayer, delegate to God a responsibility He delegated to us. Do you see what I am saying? "Whosoever" does not apply to everyone. "Anything" does not mean "everything."

As Jesus often said, *"If you have ears to hear, hear."* The truth will not destroy your faith; it will make you free (John 8:32). Doubt, frustration, unbelief, anger, and depression are often the result of holding on to a part of the truth.

Let me illustrate. Suppose you are working for a homebuilder, a man for whom you have worked many years. You trust the man completely. In fact, he has never once given you any reason to believe he would lie to you. So one day, you show up for work and this good man, who is your boss, says to you, "I want you to pick up the materials necessary to build a wall between the dining and living room area on job number 24. Here are the plans and you have the address. If you need anything, just give me a call on your phone, and I will be right out." After a while, you are on the job building the wall you were instructed to build; suddenly, you begin to think about what the boss said: "If you need anything, call me." Then you say, John is an honest man, and I know he meant what he said. I think I'll give him a call. So, you call John and the conversation goes something like this: "John, do you remember saying to me just before I left to do this wall on 24, that if I need anything to give you a call?"

John answers, "Sure, I remember; what do you need?"

You respond, "John, I need a new pick-up truck."

Do you think John's "anything" included a new pick-up truck? Of course not! It was a qualified "anything." Anything required to complete the work he commissioned.

God's "anything" is limited. He will provide anything required to complete the mission He has sent us to accomplish. However, that does not include everything that may come to mind. He is not just doing construction jobs; He is building construction workers. *"Therefore, my beloved, as you have always obeyed, not as in my presence only, but now much more in my absence, work out your own salvation with fear and trembling; ¹³for it is God who works in you both to will and to do for His good pleasure"* (Philippians 2:12-13).

We must pray: "Lord, Your will and Your kingdom are the most important things. Help me do what you have told me to do. Equip me with the tools to build the things You have put in my heart to build." Whatever I need to do the work He commanded me to do will be supplied. Yet, those things may not come until we have expended all of our personal resources. When we have come to our end, God begins.

Paul said, *"My God shall supply all your need according to His riches in glory by Christ Jesus"* (Philippians 4:19). It does not say all wants and desires will be supplied—only needs. Many of us have unrealistic expectations because they are built on false assumptions that produce false hope. Solomon said, "Hope deferred makes the heart sick" (Proverbs 13:12). God has not promised to be all things to all men. He has not committed Himself to doing everything we ask. If we are going to be effective in prayer we must learn to pray in Jesus' name.

PRAY IN JESUS' NAME

This teaching is right in line with Jesus' words: *"Whatever you ask in My name, I will do, that the Father may be glorified in the son. If you ask anything in My name, I will do it"* (John 14:13, 14). What a powerful, seemingly all-inclusive verse of Scripture, but the qualifying clause is *"ask in My name."*

I was considering this promise one day while praying, remembering the various teachings on the passage I had either heard or read. One brother said, *"It is as though Jesus has given us a blank check on the bank of heaven and has instructed us to fill it out in any amount and present it to be cashed."* Well, I had done that and my checks had bounced.

Another said, *"Jesus has given us "power of attorney"; we have the authority to use His name to get what we need."*

Suddenly I said out loud, "Lord, that does not work. I've asked things in Jesus' name and they have not been done."

I had no sooner spoken when the Father gently said, "Son, you do not know what it means to ask in Jesus' name."

I immediately began to ponder His words. As I thought about it, I knew He was right. I did not know how to ask in Jesus' name. All I was doing was presenting my "want list" and then saying, "In Jesus' name, amen." It seemed to me that I was using that name without any real understanding of what it meant. I knew, from past experience that when my Father says, "You don't know," it doesn't mean He is about to tell me. Rather, He was saying study this; find out what it means. So, I got down my interlinear *Greek New Testament* and *Thayer's Greek-English Lexicon* and searched for understanding. To my surprise, a thorough study revealed—if expanded to its fullest meaning in English—Jesus was in effect saying, "Whatever you ask by My command and authority, acting in My behalf, for the advancement of My kingdom, I will do, that the Father may be glorified in the Son."

To pray in Jesus' name took on a new meaning. His will and kingdom were to be the primary focus. I can see it; can you? As His disciples, we have been authorized to act on His behalf for the advancement of His kingdom.

When the sheriff of a given county deputizes, he is given power (gun) and authority (badge). All deputies know they do not have the authority to act in their own behalf. They must not impose their own will on others except according to the law. They must act on behalf of the one who gave them the authority. Likewise, our

King has given us authority to act on His behalf, not ours. Hence, we must not use the power given us to satisfy our selfish desires, not even our needs.

JESUS' EXAMPLE

After Jesus was baptized by John in the River Jordan, He was led by the Spirit into the wilderness to be tested by Satan (Matthew 4:1). Jesus spent forty days in the wilderness of Judea without food. Obviously, at the end of those days, He was hungry. While Jesus was in this weakened condition, Satan came to Him and said, *"Since You are the Son of God, command that these stones become bread"* (Matthew 4:3, author's paraphrase). Jesus certainly had the power to do what Satan suggested. And He could have used it to fulfill His own personal need, but He refused to do so. He said to Satan, *"Man shall not live by bread alone, but by every word that proceeds from the mouth of God"* (Matthew 4:4).

Simply put, Satan was tempting Jesus to use His power illegitimately. He wanted Him to exercise His power on His own behalf. On this occasion, Satan's defeat by Jesus is heard in His words and seen in His actions. Jesus seemed to be saying He would only do what His Father tells Him. He would only command the stones to be turned into bread if the Father instructed Him to. He would not do it to satisfy His own desires.

In the Gospel of John, Jesus said, *"I have not come to do my will, but the will of Him who sent me"* (John 6:38).

Shortly before His ascension, Jesus called His disciples around Him and told them, *"As the Father has sent me, I also send you [in the very same manner, with the very same authority"* (John 20:21). Then, as He breathed upon them, He said, *"Receive the Holy Spirit"* (John 20:22). I believe they were immediately born again. Life from above flowed into them. Straightaway, they were empowered to live as Jesus lived. A few days later, they were anointed to do the things Jesus did through the indwelling presence of the Holy Spirit. Jesus had said the Holy Spirit is with you, but now He shall be in you.

It may seem that I am overemphasizing the point, but if prayer is to be a meaningful experience, prayers must understand we are in this world to act on behalf of the One who called us. If prayer is to be truly effectual, it must be unselfish. James, our Lord's brother, said, *"You ask and receive not because you ask out of wrong motives, that you may satisfy your own selfish desires"* (James 4:3, author's paraphrase)

PRAYER

Father, we pray, Thy will be done, not my will be done. You have all wisdom and power. You know what to do, when, and how to do it. Our greatest desire is to pray the kind of prayers You will be pleased to answer. In the authority of Jesus we pray. Amen!

Chapter Eleven

God's Covenant, Our Response

Prophets have always been controversial people—men and women sent by God to speak His word to a generation. How should Christians respond to prophetic messages of holy people? How should we respond when we hear God's voice?

GOD SPOKE—NOTHING HAPPENED

I was serving as the pastor of a growing church in Arkansas. How I loved that church! The easiest church I had ever served. There were only seventy-five members when they called me. Though I was the pastor of a larger church at the time, I felt sure the Lord wanted me to accept their call.

I preached for nearly five months without seeing one person saved. Then, on a Super Bowl Sunday, the Lord saved two people—a boy and a young, well-known, businessman. From that day, we saw people commit their lives to Jesus week after week. The building was crowded even with two Sunday morning services.

During those days, I heard God speak to me and say, "I am going to raise up a church here of a thousand members." I was sure God had spoken, so I went to the people with that word. They responded positively and soon we were constructing a larger building. Everyone anticipated the completion of that sanctuary, and when the work was finished, we moved into the new facility. We were a congregation of four hundred in a building, which seated 750 with the overflow opened and suddenly, things seemed different. The warmth people had felt in the little sanctuary wasn't there. No one had been saved in the new building. No weddings or funerals had been conducted there. Nothing good or bad had happened in that place. None of us understood these feelings, and I felt pressure to make the church grow, to make things happen.

For the first time, I attended a church-growth conference. It seemed as if we should get into the bus ministry. Churches with buses were growing—but not mine. The more I tried to build the attendance, the greater my frustration. Nothing seemed to work. The people complained. The deacons were upset with me but tried not to show it.

After nearly three years in the new building, we were still a congregation of four hundred. I began to question the word I felt I had received and eventually left the church. What a disappointment! I felt like a false prophet, and I am sure there were others who felt the same. I had somehow forgotten the words of Jesus who said: *"I will build my church"* (Matthew 16:18). He had been doing a good job until I tried to interfere. I admit, I did not know I was interfering but now I know I was. I was trying to do what Jesus said was His job. If I had been successful, I would have been proud of my accomplishments. The Lord would not have it.

The church did not grow, at least, not while I remained at the helm. Jesus will not share the glory with any of us. His word is *"Without me, you can do nothing."* (John 15:5). The lesson to learn is we must do our part and leave the rest to Jesus. And, our part is pretty clear: pray and put our trust in God. Pray as if it all depends on God. Work as if it depends on you.

My problem was I did not know how to properly respond to a prophetic word. But not only me, in my travels I have met many who suffer from the same problem. I often ask, "How many of you have received what you believe is a word from God that has not come to pass?" The response is always the about the same. Many in churches who often see prophetic gifts manifested have received "words from God" that have not come to pass, and some will never come to pass. Does this mean the person who gave the prophecy was a false prophet? I don't think so. The prophet may be a man of God and the prophecy true, but this is not the whole story. Unless there is an appropriate response on the part of the one who received the word, though true, it may not come to pass. There is an old cliché that goes like this: "God said it. I believe it, and that settles it." Sounds good, and you may have said, it but it is not true. God may have said it, and you may believe it, but that does not settle it. There is something more to do. There is an appropriate way for us to respond.

NINEVEH

To illustrate my point let's look at Jonah. God sent Jonah to Nineveh with a prophetic word: *"Yet forty days, and Nineveh shall be overthrown!"* (Jonah 3:4). The message offered no way out. Forty days, and it is all over. Jonah did not want to go to Nineveh. In spite of the direct word from God, *"Go to Nineveh"* (Jonah 1:2) Jonah got on a boat headed to Tarshish. Jonah did not want to warn the Ninevites because he knew the loving nature of God. He was sure God would not destroy them if they repented, and he wanted those enemies of Israel to be destroyed. With great reluctance, Jonah went to Nineveh (after a detour through the belly of a whale). He entered the city and gave the message.

Just as he expected, they repented. The greatest to the least of them believed the message of the prophet. Even the king laid aside his royal robes, put on sackcloth, and sat on the ash heap. The Ninevites said, *"Who can tell if God will turn and relent, and turn away from His fierce anger, so that we may not perish?"* (John 3:9).

They had no assurance repenting would help, but they decided to give it a try. They changed their attitude toward God, and He changed His mind (stated intentions). There was no change in His nature or character. He just changed His stated intentions. This is seen over and over again in the Old Testament.

Of course, Jonah was upset. He looked like a false prophet. His prophecy did not come to pass. Someone has pointed out that Jonah's prophecy of destruction came to pass later, but not in that generation. We are not responsible for the generation past or the one in the future, only the present one.

Before I discuss this further, I want to establish that God makes two kinds of promises: unconditional and conditional covenants. The Bible records a few covenants that are unconditional and irrevocable.

UNCONDITIONAL COVENANTS

Consider Malachi 3:6, where God spoke and said, *"For I am the Lord, I do not change; therefore you are not consumed, O sons of Jacob."* Note carefully what God is saying:

"Because I am God and because I do not change, you sons of Jacob are not consumed."

Why was God saying this to Israel? Because He had made an unconditional covenant with Abraham (and renewed it with Isaac and Jacob) that Israel would be blessed and a blessing to all the peoples on the earth. God's promise to Abraham was, *"I will establish my covenant between Me and you and your descendants after you in their generations, for an everlasting covenant, to be God to you and to your descendants after you"* (Genesis 17:7).

But hundreds of years had passed. Abraham's descendants were not like Abraham. They were willful, disobedient rebels. To these rebels God said, "Because I do not change, you are safe. If I did change, you would be consumed. Your sins warrant judgment, but I made a promise to Abraham, and I cannot change. If I were a fickle God—as inconsistent and changeable as you—you would be consumed. But I am God. My nature (love) and My character (holiness) never change. Therefore, you have hope."

God also made an unconditional, irrevocable covenant with Noah and his descendants: *"I will never again curse the ground for man's sake, although the imagination of man's heart is evil from his youth; nor will I again destroy every living thing"* (Genesis 8:21). Then God said, *"This is the sign of the covenant which I make between*

Me and you, and every living creature that is with you, for perpetual generations: I set my rainbow in the cloud and it shall be a sign of the covenant between Me and the earth...I will look on it (the rainbow) to remember the everlasting covenant between God and every living creature of all flesh that is on the earth" (Genesis 9:12, 13, 16). Nothing will alter this covenant because God does not change. We can depend on it. His nature and character are ever the same. This covenant is irrevocable because it is unconditional.

CONDITIONAL COVENANTS

There are other covenants that are conditional and therefore revocable. Conditional covenants are in force as long as the conditions are met. If we fail to meet the conditions, God has the option to cancel the covenant. However, His very nature often causes Him to extend a covenant even after the conditions stated therein have not been met. An example of this kind of covenant is found in Exodus 15:26. Here the Lord says, *"If you diligently heed the voice of the Lord your God and do what is right in His sight, give ear to His commandments and keep all His statutes, I will put none of the diseases on you which I have brought on the Egyptians. For I am the Lord who heals you."* Though Israel did not always meet the conditions of this covenant, God was longsuffering toward them. He sent judgment only when there was no alternative.

Many of the promise-covenants of God are conditional. They usually begin with *"If you."* The "if" factor is seen in both the Old and New Testaments. God says, *"If you will, then I will. If you do not, then I will not."*

THE POWER OF PRAYER

As I was searching the Word for answers to why a prophetic word doesn't always come to fruition, I read one of Ezekiel's prophecies against the nation of Israel:

The conspiracy of the prophets in her (Israel's) midst is like a roaring lion tearing the prey; they have devoured the people; they have taken treasure and precious things; they have made many widows in her midst. Her priests have violated My law...her princes in her midst are like wolves tearing the prey...her prophets...(say), "Thus says the Lord God," when the Lord had not spoken. The people of the land have used oppressions committed robbery, and mistreated the poor and needy" (Ezekiel 22:24-29).

What a broad indictment. The priests, princes, prophets, and people were all corrupt and guilty before God. Conditions had deteriorated to the point where something had to be done.

God is the judge of the whole earth. He gave the law and must uphold it. The sentence demanded by the law must be carried out. God was faced with what seemed to be a dilemma. He is love, and He wants to extend mercy. But He is holy and the law demands judgment. How can mercy be extended? How can God delay sending judgment? Verse Ezekiel 22:30 holds the answer: *"I sought for a man among them who would make a wall (hedge), and stand in the gap before Me on behalf of the land, that I should not destroy it; but I found no one."* That's it. If one person could have been found to intercede for these rebels, God would have extended mercy even when judgment was called for. Prayer provides a way for God to extend His mercy.

Again, it was obvious to me that through prayer, God can change things. How sad that in the case of Israel, He found no one who would pray. *"Therefore, the record says, 'I have poured out My indignation on them; I have consumed them with the fire of My wrath"* (Ezekiel 22:31). Anyone can see that this is not what God wanted to do, but He had no alternative. There was no other way.

With this truth, I searched a little deeper. Would God actually change His plan? Would He change His mind? Is the outcome of a matter determined by what God says or by how we "respond" to what He says? It was not long before I saw that the latter was the case. Things do not happen, altogether, because God says it. Rather, things happen because we respond in an appropriate manner to what He says.

At one time, God spoke to Jeremiah and said, *"Do not pray for this people, or lift up a cry or prayer for them; for I will not hear them in the time that they cry out to Me because of their trouble"* (Jeremiah 11:14). A little later, God spoke again, *"Do not pray for this people, for their good. When they fast, I will not hear their cry; and when they offer burnt offering and grain offering, I will not accept them"* (Jeremiah 14:11, 12). If these words were not enough to make it clear that He would not hear Israel's prayers or accept their worship, He spoke again and said, *"Though Moses and Samuel stood before Me, yet My mind could not be favorable toward this people. Cast them out of My sight"* (Jeremiah 15:1). However, in spite of all of these words from the Lord telling Jeremiah to cease praying, he prayed all the more. When God says don't pray, it is not the time to stop. He will not disregard the cry of the intercessor. Jeremiah knew the unchanging nature and character of God. Thus, knowing that God could change His mind about the matter, he kept praying.

Jeremiah Chapter 18 holds the key to understanding how God works. Please read verses 7 and 8 carefully: *"The instant I speak concerning a nation and concerning a kingdom, to pluck up, to pull down, and to destroy it, if that nation against whom I have spoken turns from its evil, I will relent of the disaster that I thought to bring upon it"* (Jeremiah 18:7, 8). Do you hear what God is saying? He is saying, *"If the people respond properly, I will change My mind. If they repent, I will repent and relent. It is all up to the people. It does not matter what I have said; I will change My mind—though not My nature or character."*

Now let's look at the next two verses: *"And the instant I speak concerning a nation and concerning a kingdom, to build and to plant it, if it does evil in My sight so that it does not obey My voice, then I will relent concerning the good which I said I would benefit it"* (Jeremiah 18:9, 10).

There was my answer. I began to understand why things do not always happen the way God says they will. If He says He will build a church of one thousand people, it will only happen if we are in agreement with the Word and pray until it happens. If we allow criticism, unbelief, doubt, and prayerlessness to take control, what God said will happen will not.

When God says judgment will fall upon the land, I repent for the sins of the nation and cry to God for mercy. If the prophets say, "Revival is coming," I do not wait for it to happen, if I do, it will not happen. The prayer of faith and repentance is the appropriate response to the prophetic word.

Daniel 9:2 recorded: *"I, Daniel, understood by the books (prophecies) the number of the years specified by the word of the Lord, given through Jeremiah the prophet, that He would accomplish seventy years in the desolations of Jerusalem."* Daniel knew the time for Israel's return from captivity had come. He had read it in Jeremiah's prophecy. What would he do? He could have told the captives that their days of shame were finished. He could have said, "Deliverance is on the way." But He did not. Instead, He repented for the nation of Israel. *"I set my face toward the Lord God to make request by prayer and supplications, with fasting, sackcloth, and ashes"* (Daniel 9:3). The next several verses of Daniel Chapter 9 record his prayer of repentance. He confessed and repented for the sins of the nation as though they were his own personal sins. Daniel responded correctly to Jeremiah's prophecy.

It does not matter what God has said, whether He promises blessings or warns of judgment. If we pray, He will heal our land. If we don't, He won't, even if He has said He would.

You may ask, what will such teaching do to the Word of God? I'm more concerned about what it does to one's image of God. We are not serving a molten image. Our God is not a stone. He is a living being who can be touched by our sincere prayers. He will neither change His nature or His character nor will He break His unconditional covenants. But when it comes to holding back judgment or changing His plan (His stated intention) about pouring out His wrath, nothing could please Him more. If judgment comes, it is because no one made up the hedge and stood in the gap before the Lord for the land.

My dear reader, we must pray as we have never prayed. The salvation of millions in our generation depends on divine intervention, which cannot happen unless we pray.

Some time ago, I began to align my prayer with the prophecy of Joel. You will find it in Joel 2:28-32:

> And it shall come to pass afterward That I will pour out My Spirit on all flesh; Your sons and your daughters shall prophesy, your old men shall dream dreams, your young men shall see visions. And also on My menservants and on My maidservants I will pour out My Spirit in those days.

> "And I will show wonders in the heavens and in the earth: Blood and fire and pillars of smoke. The sun shall be turned into darkness, And the moon into blood, before the coming of the great and awesome day of the LORD.

> And it shall come to pass that whoever calls on the name of the LORD shall be save.

If this is what it takes for people to recognize the Lord as the One who has the right to rule, let it happen. Let the sun be darkened and the moon turn to blood. Some will not look up until something drastic happens. I am glad God loves us enough to do what it takes to cause men to repent (turn to God). Be not deceived; God will not be disregarded, at least, not forever.

PRAYER

Let it happen, Lord. Let these signs begin. Stir the hearts of those who do not know You. May they cry out for mercy. Hear them Lord. Hear their cries. Save them, we pray. In the name of Jesus.

CHAPTER TWELVE

Dealing With the Problem of Doubt

What I am about to write may be one of the greatest revelations I have ever received. It is a revelation regarding prayer and the problem of doubt, which every human being on the face of the earth with a mind will sooner or later deal with. From whence comes doubt? We were not born with it. Little babies trust. They do not and will not doubt until they have reason to do so.

Doubt is a product of our experiences with people. Faith is the product of a relationship with God. Doubt and faith live side by side in all of us. Sooner or later, every believer will have a bout with doubt. Even though little babies trust, they soon learn to doubt.

They find early on that things are not always what they were told. We are not doubters by nature, but the tendency to question what we are told is an asset, not a liability. In Arkansas, we call those who do not question "gullible," which means they will buy anything. The person who does not question and doubt is destined for much disappointment and a "heap" of trouble.

At times, we are all doubters, and that's all right. In fact, it may be more of a blessing than a problem. Doubt only becomes a problem when it dominates your life. In short, doubt is no hindrance to prayer unless it keeps you from praying. Most men and women of faith wrestle with doubt sometimes. Let's take a look at a few biblical examples:

JOHN THE BAPTIST

John the Baptist is one of the best examples of a man of faith who came under the power of doubt. Scripture tells us that John was filled with the Holy Spirit from birth, which itself was miraculous. An austere, ascetic recluse, he lived in the wilderness of Judea—some believe with the Essenes who, it is believed, buried the scrolls of Scripture in caves—near the Dead Sea. One day, John saw his cousin Jesus coming toward him and cried out with a loud voice, *"Behold! The Lamb of God who takes away the sin of the world!"* (John 1:29). John knew the true identity of Jesus, His mission, and origin. At Jesus' baptism, John saw the heavens open and the Spirit come down in the form of a dove to rest upon Jesus. He heard a voice from heaven say, *"You are My beloved Son; in You I am well pleased"* (Luke 3:22). Concerning Jesus, John declared: *"He must increase, but I must decrease"* (John 3:30). John knew Jesus, perhaps better than anyone else at that time.

Soon after Jesus began His public ministry, Herod arrested John the Baptist. While in prison, he heard of the works of Jesus and sent two of his disciples with the question: *"Are You the coming One, or do we look for another?"* (Matthew 11:3). John was questioning. He was doubting. Why? It seems to have to do with his hearing about the "works" of Jesus, not the miracles but the works. Jesus' conduct troubled John and caused him to question the revelation he had received, as well as the voice he had heard. What were the works of Jesus that so troubled John?

Perhaps he had heard Jesus had attended a wedding feast in Cana. Remember, John was an anti-social recluse who would not have been caught dead at such a gathering. If that was not enough, Jesus had turned, not just a little, but barrels of water into wine. John had never touched wine. Actually, he had been commanded by God to abstain (Luke 1:56). Jesus was developing a reputation as *"a gluttonous man and a winebibber, a friend of tax collectors and sinners"* (Matthew 11:19). I am sure John fully expected Jesus to be holier and more anti-social than he was. After all, Jesus was the Son of God. He had heard the voice of God. *"This is my beloved Son."* But now, he was not living up to John's expectations. He did not fit into the dimensions of his little box. Jesus was not acting as John had expected. Doubt began to fill his mind. He needed some reassurance. It was at this point he sent two disciples to ask, *"Are you really the One?"* (Matthew 11:3).

Jesus did not answer them directly, but said, *"Go tell John…the blind receive their sight and the lame walk; the lepers are cleansed and the deaf hear; the dead are raised up and the poor have the gospel preached to them"* (Matthew 11:4-5). Then He added a little parenthetical statement: *"Blessed is he who is not offended because of Me"* (Matthew 11:6).

Yes, believers can and will doubt. All of us do at times, especially when things don't turn out the way we expected. We prayed for a loved one's healing, but she died. A preacher in whom we had great confidence failed. A fellow Christian lied to us and cheated us in a business deal. These things happen and when they do, doubt rises within us.

A DOUBTING CHURCH PRAYS

One of the most encouraging stories for doubters is found in the Acts 12:1-17. In these verses, James the apostle's martyrdom is recorded and Peter's subsequent arrest. Luke begins Chapter 12 by saying that Herod killed James with the sword and arrested Peter, intending to bring him to trial after the Passover. Herod evidently had the same fate in mind for Peter that he had for James: *"Peter was therefore kept in prison"* (Acts 12:5).

James' untimely death had sent waves of doubt through the Jerusalem church. They had fully expected him to be miraculously delivered from prison. It had happened before. Apostles were special messengers whom God would deliver; that is what the church believed and expected. But now James was dead; Peter was in prison, and Herod intended to kill him after the days of unleavened bread were over. What were they going to do?

Knowing a little about human nature, I'm sure there were different courses of action suggested by members of the church. Some probably recommended they appeal to Herod for mercy. Perhaps others suggested prayer. And that is what they did. *"But constant prayer was offered to God for him by the church"* (Acts 12:5). Strange as it may seem, there is no indication that the church prayed for James' life to be spared. Could it be that they fully expected him to be released unharmed. Had not Peter and John previously been led out of prison by an angel of the Lord? They had good reason to believe James would be released, and he was, but he was dead. The death of James the Apostle must have sent shock waves through the church of Jerusalem. Nevertheless, whatever the case may have been, a prayer meeting was called at John Mark's house for Peter's deliverance.

Scholars estimate at that time, the Jerusalem church probably had a membership of 15,000. However, those who showed up for prayer could get into John Mark's house. He either had a large abode or the number was small. I think the latter was the case. Yet, the few people there prayed for about three days and nights bringing miraculous results.

In the middle of the night, an angel unbound Peter, led him out of the prison and disappeared. When Peter realized he was not having a dream or seeing a vision but that he was, in fact, outside the prison, he made his way to John Mark's house. Once there, he knocked on the locked gate that enclosed the courtyard of the dwelling where prayer was taking place. Rhoda, a young girl, responded to his knock. When she recognized the voice of Peter, she got so excited she forgot to unlock the gate. Quickly, she ran into the prayer meeting where with bated breath she announced, "Peter is at the gate" (Acts 12:13).

Notice the response of these faithful pray-ers: "Have you lost your mind?" One bright fellow said, "It is his angel" implying that Peter had been executed and his spirit had stopped to say good-bye before going on to glory (Acts 12:15). Are these not the words of doubters? Yes, praying doubters but doubters, nonetheless. When their prayer was answered, they couldn't believe it. How many times have I prayed about a matter and when the answer came said, "I can't believe it"? Have you ever made such a statement? God hears and answers the prayers of honest doubters.

PETER'S BOUT WITH DOUBT

Great crowds were following Jesus at this period of His ministry. On one occasion after He had fed and dismissed the people who were following Him, He instructed His disciples to cross the Sea of Galilee where He would later meet them. Jesus then went up to the top of the mountain where He spent the night in prayer. The disciples, attempting to follow the Lord's instructions, were making little progress rowing against the contrary winds. It was the fourth watch of the night and very dark when suddenly, one of them spotted a white clad figure some distances from the boat walking toward them on the water. Being fishermen and a bit superstitious, they immediately assumed they were seeing a ghost and were about to abandon ship when they heard a familiar voice, *"Don't be afraid; it is I"* (Matthew 14:27). Recognizing the voice, Peter responded, *"Lord if that is you, bid me come to you on the water*" (Matthew 14:18). Jesus said, *"Come."* Before Peter thought about what he was doing, he was over the side of the boat walking on the water toward Jesus. He was doing the impossible.

I've always wondered what the disciples in the boat were thinking. Being a man, I think I might know. "He won't make it," I hear one of them say with others joining in. Another said, "That Peter is always acting on an impulse; he is just a big show off." And all of them were probably secretly hoping he would sink and drown because if he did, they would look so much the wiser for having stayed in the safety of the boat. Isn't that the way we think? When someone takes a step of faith and begins to do the impossible, others are hoping he will fail. What should they have been saying? "Go for it, Peter! You are doing good. Don't set your eyes on the waves; just keep them on Jesus." Yes, that is what they should have been saying, but not many respond in that manner.

Peter suddenly comes to himself and sees the mighty waters around him. He is filled with fear and doubt. He cries out, *"Jesus save me!"* (Matthew 14:30). Doubt is taking him down, but faith is calling out to the One who can save him. Jesus was there immediately. He took him by the hand, stabilized him, and they walked together toward the boat. As they walked, Jesus asked, *"Why did you doubt?"* (Matthew 14:31).

Peter is not known as one who had nothing to say. In fact, on one occasion, it is written concerning him, *"Having nothing to say, he said."* But, not this time because the question Jesus asked him is unanswerable.

Things can be going great. We can be doing the impossible when suddenly, from out of nowhere, doubtful thoughts fill our minds, and we begin to sink. At this point, many question: "Will God hear such a doubter?" The answer is yes. God will hear the prayers of the honest, humble doubter. Yes, Lord, I doubt, but I also have faith. I will not allow the doubt in my head to dominate the faith in my heart. God is and God can. I am going to pray that He will meet this need. He will. He will. He will.

Jesus asked, *"Who do you say that I am?"* With positive faith Peter said: *"You are the Christ, the Son of the living God"* (Matthew 16:15, 16). Later on, this same Peter denied even knowing Jesus. The night of Jesus' arrest, doubt and fear overruled Peter's faith but at other times, his faith overcame doubt.

PETER'S FAITH OVERCOMES DOUBT

One day, Peter and his partners were washing their nets after a bad night of fishing, and Jesus asked permission to use Peter's boat as a platform for teaching the people. After He finished speaking, Jesus said to Peter, *"Launch out into the deep and let down your nets for a catch"* (Luke 5:4). Peter had a decision to make. Reason and experience told him that the effort would be fruitless. He and his partners had fished all night and had caught nothing. Besides, if Jesus knew anything about fishing, He would not have told experienced fishermen to fish in the deep in the daytime: fish were running in the shallows at night. Such thoughts must have been in Peter's mind; yet, he said, *"Nevertheless, at Your word I will let down the net"* (Luke 5:5).

In effect, Peter was saying, "It won't do any good. We won't catch anything, but I will let down the net simply because my Lord has instructed me to do so." Peter obeyed, not anticipating what was about to happen. In obedience to the Lord's command, they launched the net. As they drew it in, they could feel by its weight that it was full. Peter called James and John, his partners in the business, and they loaded both boats. They caught so many fish the two boats were about to sink. When the catch was secured, Peter fell down before the Lord and said, *"Depart from me, for I am a sinful man, O Lord"* (Luke 5:8). It is not recorded, but I am sure Peter didn't expect to catch a thing. But he ended up with so much fish, the boats almost sank. What can we learn from Peter's experience? If you have enough faith to pray and obey—even when you doubt that it will do any good—your prayer and obedience will make a great difference.

WILL GOD HEAR A DOUBTER'S PRAYER?

Obviously, God does answer doubters' prayers. The prayers at John Mark's house were offered by doubters; they were not sure God would deliver Peter. However, they knew He could and decided to pray about the matter. God did the rest.

I've heard some Bible teachers say, "You have to believe God *will* do what you ask Him." Based on Scripture, I must respectfully say, that is not true. Let me give you more examples to support my claim.

One day, a leper came to Jesus crying, *"If You are willing, You can make me clean"* (Mark 1:40). Essentially, that leper was saying, "I don't know if You will, but I know You can." To paraphrase Jesus' answer, He said, "That's good enough. If you believe I can, I will."

Another time, Jesus said to two blind men, "Do you believe I am able to do this?" Their response was, "Yes,

Lord." When He saw they believed He was able, He healed them (Matthew 9:28).

Such is the faith of Abraham. In Romans 4:20, 21, we read that Abraham *"did not waver at the promise of God. Being fully convinced that what He had promised He was also able to perform."* You only have to believe God can and determine to pray that He will until the matter is resolved.

These followers of Jesus and pray-ers of the first church of Jerusalem had enough faith to pray. They did not let doubt dominate their lives. Remember doubt is a hindrance to prayer only if it keeps you from praying.

CHAPTER THIRTEEN

How Much Faith Does It Take to Please God?

Hebrews 11:6 says, *"Without faith (in some amount) it is impossible to please Him (God)."* Romans 14:23 says, *"Whatever is not from faith is sin."* These are strong words. Faith is essential; we cannot please God without some amount of it. The writer of Hebrews does not tell us how much faith it takes to please God—just that if we don't have it, we cannot possibly please Him.

Most Christians believe they need more faith than they have. But it is my conviction that most people have more faith than they think. They often exercise faith without knowing it.

Paul says in Romans 12:3, *"God has dealt (given) to each one (believer) a measure of faith."* Once, the disciples prayed, *"Lord, increase our faith"* (Luke 17:5). Though some believers, like Stephen, were "full" of faith (Acts

6:5), others were described as "weak" in faith (Romans 14:1). From these and other verses of Scripture, we can see that there are different quantities and qualities of faith. In the Gospels, Jesus identified different levels of faith.

Little Faith

To those who were worried about whether or not they would have food to eat or clothing to wear, He said, *"O you of little' faith"* (Matthew 6:30). To His disciples who were afraid they were going to be shipwrecked, He said, *"O you of little faith"* (Matthew 8:26). Jesus used that phrase again with Peter when he began to sink while walking on the water toward Him (Matthew 14:23-33). Catching him by the hand, Jesus pointed out that Peter's problem, in addition to doubt, was *"little' faith."*

On another occasion, when His disciples were concerned they had no bread, Jesus spoke again about the smallness of their faith (Matthew 16:8). This time, He referred to their lack of understanding of spiritual truth.

Great Faith

In contrast, the Canaanite woman who pleaded for her daughter's deliverance was said to have *"great"* faith (Matthew 15:28). And to the centurion who believed Jesus could heal his servant just by speaking the word,

Jesus said, *"I have not found such great faith, not even in Israel!"* (Matthew 8:10).

In Matthew Chapter 13, in the parable of the sower, Jesus identified four kinds of soil. Matthew 13:3-23). Faith is like a seed planted in the soil of a soul. This seed of faith has the potential to grow, and under the proper conditions, it may grow quite rapidly. Some circumstances and conditions are conducive to the growth and development of faith. On the other hand, some conditions are not at all conducive.

The seed of faith has the potential to grow; yet, it does not do so at the same rate in all of us. Even the good soil did not produce its yield at the same rate. In fact, under certain conditions and circumstances, seed planted in good soil will hardly grow. This is true in the natural realm, and anything that is true in the natural realm has its parallel truth in the spiritual realm. Extremely dry conditions, storms, and weeds can retard growth even though nothing is wrong with the seed, the sower, or the soil.

From experience, I have learned that the level and quality of faith cannot be determined by one's ability to prophesy, heal the sick, do miracles, or cast out devils. Hear the words of Jesus recorded in Matthew 7:21-23:

Not all who sound religious are really godly people. They may refer to Me as 'Lord,' but they still won't get to heaven. For the decisive element is whether or not they obey the Father in heaven. At the judgment many will tell Me, 'Lord, Lord, we told others about You and used Your name to cast out demons and to many other great miracles. 'But I will reply, "You have never been Mine. Go away, for your deeds are evil'" (author's paraphrase).

FAITH'S BEST EVIDENCE

Your testimony is not the best evidence of faith. Obedience to God's Word and positive action based on a true conviction He will and can do anything He promised are faith's best evidence.

A story in Mark Chapter 2 has always intrigued me. Jesus was teaching in a certain house in Capernaum. A crowd of people gathered in the house and when it was full, they filled the yard surrounding it. It was under such difficult conditions that these four men carried their paralytic friend to the Lord to be healed. No room was inside or out. Confronted with such a situation, many would have been discouraged and given up—but not these men. Their friend's only hope was in the middle of that crowd, and they had to get him into the presence of Jesus. The only way seemed to be through the roof of the house. It was no small task, but despite the difficulty they defiantly got their friend onto the roof and began breaking a hole through the tile.

Can you imagine what was happening down below? Dirt and debris were falling on the crowd of people, and they were not pleased. Eventually, four faces appeared in the opened hole and down came a man on his bed into the presence of the Lord. Mark records that Jesus *"saw their faith."* How? Well, you can't really see faith; you can only see what it produces. Jesus called their action faith. James 2:20 says, *"Faith without appropriate action is dead"* (author's paraphrase). Unless faith is accompanied by action, it is an empty confession often based on nothing more than presumption.

Someone has rightly said "Talk is cheap." Just draw a breath of air into your lungs; put pressure on your diaphragm; release a little of that air through your vocal chords; move your lips and tongue, and you can say, "I have great faith." It does not take much to do that, but God's Word makes it clear that an empty confession is not enough. God is looking for obedience: *"Be doers of the word, and not hearers only"* (James 1:2).

If you are a Christian, you have faith. From Hebrews 11:6, we can see how much faith it takes to please God. Hear these words: *"He who comes to God must believe that He is."* To please God, you must believe that He is. Can you say with confidence, I believe God is? If you can, you have passed the first half of the test. Faith is a deep conviction that, though I have never seen Him with these fleshly eyes, He is. All of the stalwarts of faith listed in Hebrew Chapter 11 had faith and that made them different. They could all say, I believe God is, not was or will be but is. I cannot prove it, but I know God is! His name is I AM. Do you believe He is? If you do, then you have faith.

An additional characteristic of faith is given in Hebrews 11:6: *"For he who comes to God must believe…that He is a rewarder of those who diligently seek Him."* The second question on the faith test is do you believe God is a rewarder of those who diligently seek Him? I have asked that question of many people, and most of them answered with a resounding yes. Christians believe that God is, and He has the power to do what He wants to do. No one can please God without this much faith. Can you say from the heart, "I believe God rewards those who diligently seek Him?" If you can, you have enough faith to please God and thus, pray effectively.

This kind of faith moves us to action. I cannot believe God is and live as if He is not. My actions will ultimately come into line with my faith. If it is otherwise, I do not have living, active faith. I only have an empty, meaningless, hypocritical profession. James gives us a strong corrective word on this subject: *"Dear brothers, what's the use of saying that you have faith and are Christians if you aren't proving it by helping others? Will that kind of faith save anyone? It isn't enough just to have faith. You must also do good"* (James 2:14, 17, TLB).

Again, if you believe God is, and He answers those who earnestly call upon Him, you have enough faith to please God. But if that faith is not moving you to do right, you still have a long way to go. People are not displeasing God because of their lack of faith. The thing that has always displeased God is our failure to live out in our daily walk what we say we believe. Faith, real faith, followed by appropriate action is the thing that pleases Him.

WHAT IS GOD'S REWARD?

God's special favor does not rest upon transgressors. Yet, God's grace is extended toward all, the just and the unjust, good and bad. All receive sunshine and rain, seedtime and harvest. People do not live because they are good or die because they are bad. Both good and bad enjoy the same opportunities. Recently, a man who was showing me his property said to me, "The Lord has surely been good to me." My response was, "The harder and smarter one works, the more that person seems to be blessed." He was a hard-working, diligent man, and he had material things to show for it. However, the things he had did not come as an indication of God's special favor upon his life. The things he had were the reward of his own personal efforts.

You may disagree with that statement, but please hear me. Yes, I thank the Lord every day for the grace that He has bestowed upon us all. He created us in His image and likeness. Something of the divine is in all of us: good or bad, obedient or disobedient. We have the potential to succeed or fail.

Too often, we blame God or the Devil for things that are our own doing. And we shouldn't assume that wealthy, seemingly successful people are necessarily walking in God's special favor.

I was in Washington, D.C. working with a realtor who was helping me find property suitable for the National Prayer Embassy. The man was from India, and he'd come to America with eight dollars and seven pounds of clothing. He'd taken a job handling newspapers, working his way through school. That man is now one of the top men in a very large company. He is not a Christian. Has his success come as a result of God's special favor? I think not. My dad had only a third-grade education. In spite of his educational deficiency, through hard work and diligence, he established his own business and lived in retirement for more than thirty years on the fruit of his labors. Given the right opportunity, most of us have the ability to get wealth.

All five of my father's sons—raised under the same circumstances with the same parents—had essentially the same opportunities. Yet, we do not all have the same material wealth. If God's special favor can be measured in terms of material wealth, one would have to conclude that God's special favor comes to the unjust more that the just, to the unfaithful rather than the faithful. God's approval on our lives cannot be determined by the quantity of our material possessions.

Without faith, we cannot please God regardless of what we do. On the other hand, we cannot please Him with a faith that does not move us to right doing. And if we try to measure the favor of God by what we possess, we will live in constant confusion.

Sometime ago, I was walking through a new home of a friend. It was nice—a real mansion—and I said to the Lord, "You have really blessed my friend."

I was surprised when the Lord responded, "This is not My blessing."

"Well, Lord," I said, "That's what we have always said."

"You don't have anything like this, do you?" He replied.

"Well, no, I don't."

Then God asked, "Do you think I love your friend more than I love you?"

"No, Lord, I know You love me as much as You love him."

God continued, "I do not bless My people with these kinds of things. My blessings are spiritual blessings."

Then I remembered the words of Paul: *"Blessed be the God and Father of our Lord Jesus Christ, who has blessed us with all 'spiritual' blessings in heavenly places in Christ"* (Ephesians 1:3).

The Lord said to me, "Material wealth comes to Christians to test their integrity and character. If they use their wealth selfishly, they fail the test."

God does not send special favor upon the selfish and self-centered. My friend has wealth because he has worked hard, taken advantage of opportunities and handled his money wisely. It was not the special favor of God. If he does not use his wealth properly, he will answer to God.

As Christians, we are slaves of the Master whose name is Jesus. When I work, it is for Him. When I invest, it is not for me; it is for Him. I have been given some talents to hold or invest in on His behalf. If I become possessive or claim ownership, I have lost sight of my stewardship.

Obedience is better than sacrifice or worship (1 Samuel 15:22). That is what Samuel said to Saul as he returned home with the spoils of battle and the captured King Agag. His orders had been to destroy everything, but Saul made a decision to disobey. He had a better plan—much more reasonable and logical; it eventually cost him the kingdom.

Wise Solomon knew that *"There is a way which seems right to a man, but its end is the way of death"* (Proverbs 14:12). God is not interested in our worship if we are walking in disobedience. We must repent and turn from our ways to His. He will forgive, and His special favor can be upon us once again.

The longer I live, the firmer I have come to believe most of the things that happen in life are the results of natural law. It is a principle established by God: actions have consequences. It is the same for believers and nonbelievers. God does not interfere unless He is requested to do so. He waits for us to ask.

FAITH IN PRAYER OR PRAYER IN FAITH

What does all of this have to do with prayer? Faith and prayer are vitally linked—not faith in prayer but faith in God. If you believe God is and God can, and if you are walking in obedience to His Word, you are ready to pray. Pray with faith in God, not with faith in prayer.

H. Clay Trumball, in his little book *"Prayer"* written nearly a hundred years ago, said:

There is a vast difference between prayer in faith and faith in prayer. Faith in prayer is very common. Almost everybody has more or less of it. Prayer in faith is anything but common; so uncommon, in fact that our Lord questions if He will find any of it when He comes back again to the earth. Prayer in faith is a commanded duty; faith in prayer is not commanded, nor is it justifiable. Prayer in faith is spiritual; faith in prayer, too often, superstitious and presuming.

We must have our faith in God—not in anything we do as a religious act. It is presumptuous to think that we will be heard if we pray just right. Faith in "just right" prayer will not accomplish anything. Our faith must rest in a loving God who hears the prayers of His children and knows when and how to answer. He also knows if they should be answered.

When we pray a prayer known to be in the will of God believing it will be answered, it is. Not some of the time—every time. When we pray not knowing God's will, we ask Him to do what He deems best. As we pray with this kind of faith, we know that whatever happens, whatever the outcome, His will has been done.

Much of the time, our faith in God is not lacking. Rather our problem lies in the fact that we are trying to have faith in ourselves. We mistakenly think we need to pray better prayers to be heard. But faith, if it is to be effective, must rest solely upon the Lord. It must rest in His goodness, not in ours, as I have said before. We must be obedient, but we must not trust in our obedience. We must be righteous, but we cannot trust our righteousness to open heaven to our prayers.

Jesus made this very clear in His story to some who boasted of their virtue:

Two men went up to the temple to pray, one a Pharisee and the other a tax collector. The Pharisee stood and prayed thus with himself: "God, I thank you that I am not like other men—extortionist, unjust, adulterers, or even as this tax collector. I fast twice a week; I give tithes of all that I possess." And the tax collector, standing afar off, would not so much as raise his eyes to heaven, but beat his breast, saying, "God be merciful to me a sinner!" I tell you, this man went down to his house justified rather than the other. (Luke 18:10-14)

In the eyes of man, the Pharisee was righteous but in the eyes of God, he was a sinner. On another occasion, Jesus said, *"Many who are first will be last, and the last first"* (Matthew 19:30).

Spiritual pride and haughtiness will not only separate us from people, these things also put a barrier between God and us. James warns us: *"God…sets Himself against the proud and haughty"* (James 4:6, TLB).

Perhaps we do not need more faith in God or ourselves. What we need is greater faithfulness— faithfulness in the place of prayer, faithfulness in the place of worship and praise, faithfulness in the home and workplace. God places a high premium on faithfulness. Heaven's rewards are not promised to the successful but to the faithful. Those who seek God with pure hearts will find Him.

IS PHYSICAL HEALING DEPENDENT ON GREAT FAITH?

While I'm discussing this matter of faith, let me touch upon prayer for healing. I cannot tell you why God heals one and does not heal another. To say that it is His will to heal everyone, every time, does not seem to measure up to the way things really are. It has been my experience that God, at present, heals some of the people some of the time. Faith, though required to please God, seems to have little to do with it. I have seen people healed who confessed to having no faith. I have seen people who seemed to have deep faith receive no positive response to their prayers.

Why are Christians who believe in divine healing sick? It is not necessarily because they have sinned, lost faith, displeased God, or that He does not heal today. Christians are sick for many of the same reasons others are sick. They were born with physical weaknesses; they have disregarded the laws that govern health; they hold unforgiveness in their hearts; jealousy, bitterness, resentment, and fear have weakened their immune systems; low self-esteem and feelings of guilt have produced anxiety.

What is the appropriate response to God's promise *"I am the Lord who heals you"* (Exodus 15:16)"? What about *"By His stripes we are healed* (Isaiah 53:5)"? Receive them; believe them. Pray and receive prayer for divine healing with faith that God can do what you are asking. And if He does not, He is still God. Know that what happens as you pray is the will of God for your life. We must do what we believe we should, and have the attitude of Esther who said, *"If I perish, I perish"* (Esther 4:16). I do not always know what is going to happen when I pray. Often I am surprised at the answers; yet, I have a made-up mind: I will pray as long as there is life. And in death as in life, I will say, "Nevertheless, Thy will be done."

I hear someone asking, but what about the suffering? Isn't God concerned about pain and death? Does He want His people to suffer?

Scripture is clear about God's attitude toward the death of a saint: *"Precious in the sight of the Lord is the death of His saints"* (Psalm 116:15). Though it is not always easy to see the benefits of suffering, we must believe there are some. Paul said he sought the Lord three times about a problem in his flesh. Then the Lord spoke to him and said, *"No, I will not take away the thorn, but I am with you, and that is all you need. My power shows up best in weak people"* (2 Corinthians 12:7-10). Paul learned to say, *"When I am weak, then I am strong"* (2 Corinthians 12:10). The less we have the more we depend on Him.

Recently, I had the opportunity of having lunch with a pastor friend who, though in good health, had a stroke. He could not speak or call his wife or children by name. He had to learn much of Scripture again and relearn the meaning of words. A thousand members left his church in confusion and frustration. He believed in divine healing, preached and taught it, but did not seem to experience it. Hear the testimony of my friend. "I thank God for the physical difficulty I have been through. I know Him now at a level I had never known Him." His experience was humbling and in so many words, that's exactly what happened to him through the physical trial. He was humbled and came to know God in a more meaningful way. By the way, God has added another thousand to His church as well.

We must not allow the Enemy or the teachings of some well-meaning Christians to blind our eyes to the wonders of God that often come through suffering. Greater praise to God comes from those who are delivered out of troubles than those who are shielded from trouble, trial, or sickness. The mentality of the early church toward trials and persecution can be seen in Acts 5:41: *"The Apostles rejoiced that they had been counted worth of suffering and disgrace for the Name."* Paul said in his letter to the Roman Christians, *"I consider that the sufferings of this present time are not worthy to be compared with the glory which shall be revealed in us"* (Romans 8:18). He added, *"All things work together for good to those who love God"* (Romans 8:28).

In the midst of trouble, Romans 8:28 is hard to believe but looking back from the mountaintop of victory, we can understand it. Every turn in the road was important. Every obstacle overcome made us stronger. Each thing built upon another was needed to bring us to the place we are now. Some of us who are older can look down from the top and say, *"Come on, you are going to make it."* To those who are about to lose heart, we have been where you are. We made it and so can you: *"Let us not grow weary while doing good, for in due season we shall reap it we do not lose heart"* (Galatians 6:9).

PRAYER

Father, I pray for those who are going through heavy trials. Let them know You are an ever-present help in the time of trouble. Put praise in their mouths. Restore the joy of their salvation. Bring Your peace, I pray. Amen!

CHAPTER FOURTEEN

Lord, Teach Us to Pray

One day, Jesus was praying in a certain place. When he finished, one of His disciples said to Him, *"Lord, teach us to pray, just as John taught his disciples"* (Luke 11:1). What an interesting request: *"Lord, teach us to pray."* This is what this disciple wanted most of all. He could have said: "Lord, teach us to heal, do miracles, open blind eyes, and raise the dead." He had seen Jesus do all of these things, but his request was teach us to pray. He obviously realized that Jesus had something he did not have and believed it was connected to His prayer life. Jesus had an intimate relationship with His Father. As I wrote at the beginning of this book, the primary purpose of prayer is to develop a meaningful relationship with the Father through communion, which always includes communication: a two-sided conversation.

This disciple had often seen Jesus arise early in the morning, leave the disciples, go out to a quiet place and pray. On other occasions, he saw Jesus leave the crowd, go up on a mountain and spend the night in prayer. He seemed to have reached the conclusion that the ministry of Jesus was connected to His prayer life. Jesus went from one prayer place to another and in between, He ministered to the needs of the people. The pattern was obvious. This disciple could see it and consequently prayed, Lord, teach us to pray. To this request, Jesus gave a very clear answer that needs little explanation. He simply said: *"When you pray say..."* (Luke 11:2).

Pay attention! These are not the words of a novice. They are the words of none other than the only begotten Son of the Father, Creator of heaven and the earth. He, Jesus, Savior said: *"When you pray say..."* What were they to say? "Our Father."

"OUR FATHER..."

Thirteen times in Matthew Chapter 6, where this prayer was first recorded, Jesus refers to God as Father. You will not find God referred to as Father anywhere in the King James Version of the Old Testament. Yet, here in this one chapter, Jesus calls Him Father 13 times. And the New Testament abounds with references to God as Father. It is absolutely essential that we relate to God as our Father. It was God's ultimate purpose in creation to display His Fatherhood. Jesus was His one and only Son.

In his book, *God's Ultimate Intention*, DeVerne Fromke states that it was God's ultimate intention to have many sons who would be just like Jesus. Paul says in Romans Chapter 8:29: *"For those God foreknew he also predestined to be conformed to the likeness of his Son, that he might be the firstborn among many brothers"* (NIV). "God chose us out from among all the others and marked us out to be exact duplicates of His son, Jesus" (author's translation). Jesus was the first born of many sons. We shall be like Him, for we shall see Him as He is (1 John 3:2, 3).

He has given some apostles, and some prophets, and some evangelists, and some shepherds and teachers, ¹²for the perfecting of the saints; with a view to [the] work of [the] ministry, with a view to the edifying of the body of Christ; ¹³until we all arrive at the unity of the faith and of the knowledge of the Son of God, at [the] full-grown man, at [the] measure of the stature of the fullness of the Christ (Ephesians 4:11).

God is our Father. We must keep in mind all things began with Him and will find their completion in Him. He will be all and in all (1 Corinthians 15:28). It has always been God's intention to have many sons, and He will finish the work He started. Our business is to recognize who He is and to know the earth was not created for us, but for Him. Paul prays in Ephesians 1:15-23:

> *Wherefore I also, having heard of the faith in the Lord Jesus which [is] in you, and the love which [ye have] towards all the saints, ¹⁶do not cease giving thanks for you, making mention [of you] at my prayers, ¹⁷that the God of our Lord Jesus Christ, the Father of glory, would give you [the] spirit of wisdom and revelation in the full knowledge of him, ¹⁸being enlightened in the eyes of your heart, so that ye should know what is the hope of his calling, [and] what the riches of the glory of his inheritance in the saints, ¹⁹and what the surpassing greatness of his power towards us who believe, according to the working of the might of his strength, ²⁰[in] which he wrought in the Christ [in] raising him from among [the] dead, and he set him down at his right hand in the heavenlies, ²¹above every principality, and authority, and power, and dominion, and every name named, not only in this age, but also in that to come; ²²and has put all things under his feet, and gave him [to be] head over all things to the assembly, ²³which is his body, the fullness of him who fills all in all.*

We are here for Him. We were redeemed for Him. We are saved for Him. We are obedient for Him. We live for Him. He does not live for us. We are not the center of creation. He is!

"OUR"

Note the plural pronoun "our." It is an all-inclusive word. Religion is exclusive; it always has been and always will be. God is our Father—the Father of all the elect. Our unity is in Him. There can be no true unity apart from Him. He is *our* Father—Father of Afro-American, Spanish, Oriental, Native American, and all believers. He cannot be *my* Father until He is *our* Father. He is not the Father to those who are exclusive.

There has been much talk about unity in the body of Christ. Many attempts have been made to accomplish this worthy goal. However, it seems to me that we should recognize our unity, instead of trying to find it. Our unity is in our Father, not in our faith. We are all at different levels of faith and understanding. This is not that important. This is the Father's business. He is patiently waiting for us to recognize our sonship and His Fatherhood; then and then alone will we know unity.

"In heaven," our Father is above all, over all, in control of all, sees all, hears all, and knows all. He is sovereign. He loves His children and has invited us to come into His presence. What an honor. *"Call unto me and I will answer you"* (Jeremiah 33:3). This is His promise to us. *"Ask and you shall receive"* (Matthew 7:7).

God has given us great and precious promises. Enter His presence with confidence. Once and for all, He has settled the sin problem, which separated us from Him. *"For by one offering he has perfected in perpetuity the sanctified"* (Hebrews 10:14, Darby's translation). *"By one sacrifice he has made perfect forever those who are being made holy"* (Hebrews 10:14, NIV).

Therefore, we can come boldly to the throne of grace. Our approach is not with fear and anxiety. It is with confidence, great respect, and unfeigned gratitude that He has made and is making us, through the Holy Spirit, exact duplicates of His only begotten.

"HALLOWED BE THY NAME..."

"Hallowed be Thy name" is the first praise and worship part of the prayer Jesus taught this disciple. Once we focus on who God is, who we are, our relationship with Him and all others, we can worship with a pure heart and motives. This is where I spend a lot of my time in prayer. Our relationship with Him grows and develops as we worship Him in Spirit and in truth.

"THY KINGDOM COME..."

At this point in prayer, we present our first petition. What is your deepest desire? Does it line up with His? Do you really want His kingdom to come? Or are you more interested in your kingdom? God knows. We can't con Him.

What does this mean? What will it be like here on the earth when the kingdom of God is established? Scripture gives us a glimpse of what it will be like when His kingdom is established on the earth. The entire earth will worship God.

> *"All the ends of the world Shall remember and turn to the LORD, and all the families of the nations shall worship before You"* (Psalm 22:27).

> *"And the earth shall worship You and sing praises to You; they shall sing praises to Your name"* (Psalm 65:4).

> *"All nations whom You have made shall come and worship before You, O Lord and shall glorify Your name"* (Psalm 85:9).

> *Now it shall come to pass in the latter days that the mountain of the LORD'S house shall be established on the top of the mountains, and shall be exalted above the hills;*

> *And all nations shall flow to it. Many people shall come and say, "Come, and let us go up to the mountain of the LORD, to the house of the God of Jacob; He will teach us His ways, and we shall walk in His paths." For out of Zion shall go forth the law, and the word of the LORD from Jerusalem. He shall judge between the nations, and rebuke many people; They shall beat their swords into plowshares,*

And their spears into pruning hooks; nation shall not lift up sword against nation, neither shall they learn war anymore. O house of Jacob, come and let us walk in the light of the LORD. (Isaiah 2:2-5).

Daniel interprets Nebuchadnezzar's dream.

"And in the days of these kings the God of heaven will set up a kingdom which shall never be destroyed; and the kingdom shall not be left to other people; it shall break in pieces and consume all these kingdoms, and it shall stand forever" (Daniel 2:38).

I was watching in the night visions,

My greatest desire is to see God's kingdom established on the earth, and I pray for this with a clear understanding that I am praying according to His eternal plan. *"Ask me, and I will give you the nations for your inheritance and uttermost parts of the earth as your possession."* (Psalm 2:9, KJV).

There are literally scores of Scriptures that describe the kingdom of God, which is to ultimately be revealed.

PRAYER

Father, may Your kingdom come. Let it be established on the earth as it is in heaven. This is Your plan. It has been from the beginning. I set my heart and mind to agree with Your expressed will.

"YOUR WILL BE DONE..."

With the words, "Your will be done," we surrender our wills to His. We do this with the knowledge that His will is best for us, our loved ones, and our Father. Great peace is the fruit of full surrender to the Father's will. His will is more important than an answer to my prayers, which may only be a manifestation of my will. Be fully convinced that His will is best.

Let me refer once again to a book by DeVerne Fromke entitled, *Life's Ultimate Privilege* (Sure Foundations Publishers). In this book, Mr. Fromke points out that God is someone greater than an answerer. He wants us to know Him, not only as One with whom we can share our needs and concerns. But He also wants us to know Him intimately and personally and to participate with Him in His eternal purpose. He wants us to become partners with Him in all His ways. When we know Him as Father, we will be more concerned about His will than ours.

"GIVE US THIS DAY...OUR DAILY BREAD"

We cannot pray today for tomorrow's need. This is a day-to-day walk. Israel could not gather a two-day supply of manna, except on Fridays. We need to connect with God on a daily basis. He is ever present, a fact we must not lose sight of. He wants us to live with a continual awareness of His presence. We do not have to be repetitive, but we do need to be ever conscious. He is there. If I speak, He will hear. If He speaks, I will hear. We are not trying to become so blessed that we no longer need God daily.

I have observed those who when they had little or nothing depended on the Lord. However, once they had more than they needed, they forgot the One who gave to them. Father, let it not be true of us. We want to live with a continual awareness of Your presence.

Will our Father always meet our needs? Absolutely! What about our wants and desires? Those He meets as we are mature enough to receive them.

"FORGIVE US... AS WE FORGIVE"

There will be little assurance of forgiveness until we forgive. Our Father will see to it. We must forgive those who have wronged us. This is a prayer to be prayed daily. We need God's forgiveness every day. He gladly gives the assurance of forgiveness to those who forgive.

"LEAD US...BUT NOT INTO TEMPTATION"

Our Father has blessed His children with an internal guidance system in the person of the Holy Spirit. Paul puts it this way: *"As many as are the sons of God, are led by the Spirit of God"* (Romans 8:14). Put literally, He is saying that all those who are His sons are led by the Holy Spirit whom He has given to dwell within. We have no pillar of fire or cloud, not even a voice, except the still quiet voice that comes as an internal impression. We say God spoke, but the truth is, we did not hear anything. Yet, as I have already pointed out, we know. Suddenly, those who are children of God know what to do, what to say, and where to go. We just know. Can this be proved? Probably not, but it is true, nonetheless.

We have confidence that God will not lead us where it is not right for us to go. We don't want to be led into temptation, but if He allows it, we know, this too, is the right road.

"DELIVER US FROM THE EVIL ONE."

The word "from" can be taken to mean out of the hands of the Evil One. In other words, at times I may find myself in Satan's grip, but my Father will deliver me. The Enemy set traps for us. Sometimes we see them; sometimes we don't. But of this we can be sure, our Father will not leave us in Satan's hands longer than we can endure.

God called Satan's attention to His servant Job. *"Have you considered Job, that there is none like him in all the earth?"* Satan responded, *"Job serves you because you* bless him. *Remove your blessing and he will curse You.*" God says, *"He is in your hands; do to him as you wish; only spare his life."* The book of Job tells the whole story. God showed Satan how wrong he was about Job. In all his trials and tribulations, Job refused to curse God as his wife urged and Satan desired. Instead, His response was, *"Though He slay me I will trust Him"* (Job 13:15). God does not test us so He would know the outcome. He allows us to be tested so others may know we do not love and serve Him because of what He does for us. We do so because He is our Father and deserves our love and obedience. He is a good God. Hallelujah!

"FOR YOURS IS THE KINGDOM, THE POWER AND THE GLORY."

We return to praise. We magnify our Father, His authority, His power, and His glory. I have not found a better pattern of prayer. I do not believe there is one. Jesus gave this prayer in answer to the request, *"Lord, teach us to pray."* Again, this is the response of Jesus, *"When you pray say…"* To sum it all up: everything Christians need to pray about is covered under the various points of this prayer outline:

"Our Father"—speaks of relationship.

"Which art in heaven"—reminds us of His sovereignty.

"Hallowed by thy name"— leads us to praise.

"Thy kingdom come"—puts first things in first place.

"Thy will be done"—releases everything to His control.

"Give us"—He is our source; we are needy.

"This day"—reminds us to be consistent.

"Our daily bread"—Jesus is the Bread of Life.

"Forgive us"—reminds me of my sins and His solution.

"As we forgive"—keeps me free from unforgivness.

"Lead us"—His Spirit leads.

"Not into temptation"—temptation is real

"Deliver us from the Evil One"—through Jesus I will overcome.

"Thine is the kingdom" —divine ownership

"Thine is the power"—full authority

"Thine is the glory" —return to praise

AN EXAMPLE

To show you how you might fill in this outline, I will write out this prayer exactly as I pray it. Of course, I don't say the same words every day, but I follow this pattern, which I trust will help you as much as it helped the woman I met in Virginia. This prayer will set up the conditions under which God has the option to do anything that needs to be done.

Father, You are in heaven over all the things of this earth. You see all. You are concerned about all. I thank You that I can call You my Father. You are my Father. You chose me, Father, out from among all the others, and You marked me out to be an exact duplicate of Your Son, Jesus. Thank You, Father. You cleansed me from all of my sins. I enter Your presence only because You offered a sacrifice for my sins. Through that sacrifice, I can come boldly to the throne of grace. Thank You, Father, that we do not come to a throne of judgment; we come to a throne of grace.

I will not be rejected. I am accepted in Christ Jesus, my Lord, whose blood has atoned for my sins. I come before You, not with righteousness I have attained through self-effort, but righteousness I obtained by faith, which You provide. I am accepted, not because I am good, but because You are good. You are my righteousness. Through the blood I have forgiveness of sins. Not only do I have forgiveness of sins through the blood, but I also have the fullness of the Holy Spirit.

Thank You, Father, for the indwelling presence of the person of the Holy Spirit. He is my peace. He is my glory. What a blessing it is to fellowship with Him. Thank You, Holy Spirit, for living in me. You are welcome in this temple. Take full control of every member of my body. Help me to pray with the spirit and with the understanding.

Father, thank You that my sins are forgiven and for the fullness of the Holy Spirit. Thank You that I have soundness of body through the Lord Jesus Christ. With His stripes I am healed. Thank You that healing is not only for me; it is for Your body, the church. Lord, let healing flow to Your body. Heal the wounds. Bind up the broken ones. Bring unity into Your body.

Thank You, Father, that through the sacrifice You made for us, every financial need is met. You are my provider. You are Jehovah-jireh. All my needs You have supplied according to Your riches in glory by Christ Jesus, our Lord.

And Father, I thank You for being my assurance. I will conquer every foe with You on my side. You are my Shepherd. I shall not want. You make me to lie down in green pastures. You lead me beside still waters. You restore my soul. You lead me in paths of righteousness for Your name's sake. Though I walk through the valley of the shadow of death, I will fear no evil. Your rod and Your staff comfort me. You prepare a table before me in the presence of my enemies. You anoint my head with oil. My cup is running over. Surely, goodness and mercy will follow me all the days of my life, and I will dwell in the house of the Lord, forever and forever. Hallelujah!

Every moral, spiritual, physical, financial, and emotional need is met in my Lord Jesus. Thank You, Lord, for the provision You have made. And now, Father, I pray, Thy kingdom come. Thy will be done on the earth as it is in heaven. Father, this is what I desire. I want Your kingdom, and You as King to be first in my life. No one but Jesus will rule my life this day. I surrender my whole being to Your Lordship. Let Your kingdom be established in my life. Let Your will be done in my life and family.

Lord, I lift up my family to You. I pray that each one of my brothers, children, and grandchildren will let Jesus rule their lives. And, Lord, it is not just for my family that I pray; I also pray for my church family. I pray for my pastor and all the pastors of Your church. May Your kingdom be established and Your will be done in their lives. I stand against the spirit of deception and distraction. I bind the spirit of disruption, discouragement, and destruction. And, Father, make Your pastors wise. Help them to discern the true nature of every matter. Grant them physical strength to do the work You called them to do.

Father, I pray for all those in leadership in Your church. The elders and deacons—bless and strengthen them. Grant them the ability to do what You want them to do. Minister to their families, I pray. In Jesus' name.

Not only for the pastors and leaders, Lord, I pray also for the people of Your church. I pray first for the children. Minister to the children of the church and this generation. Most of them know nothing about Jesus. Raise up strong, effective ministry to the little ones. Raise up and gift people to write and produce television materials suitable for children—programs with messages of hope that are so good and well-produced that the national networks can't reject them.

We lift up the youth to You, O Lord. Reach them, we pray. You know exactly what to do to touch each and every person for whom Jesus died. Bless and strengthen those who are ministering effectively to the youth of this generation. Supply all of their needs. Open doors for them. Send a manifestation of Your supernatural power. For their sakes, reach them, O Lord.

For the single adults, I pray. Many are hurting. Many suffer from rejection. Many have lost all confidence in themselves. Many are full of anger and bitterness. Minister to them, Lord. Help them to turn their eyes toward You. Let Your peace flow into their hearts.

And for the young married ones, I pray, Lord. They need Your help. I stand against the Enemy on their behalf. I resist the spirit of destruction that has been sent to destroy marriage relationships today. I resist the spirit of divorce and deception. In the name of Jesus.

Father, I also pray for senior adults. They need You, Lord. Many feel discouraged. Many have been neglected. Be near them, O Lord, and let them know the reality of Your holy presence.

And Father, I pray for the ministries of the church: our missionaries, evangelists, and teachers. Minister to and through them. Father, I especially pray for the pray-ers—those upon whom You have placed a desire to pray. Grant that they will never grow weary and lose heart. Help them to pray and to keep on praying until we see the spiritual awakening You promised in Your Word and through Your prophets.

Father, we pray for our nation. We repent of our national sins. We have sinned against You, O Lord. We have legalized the murder of our unborn children. I know this is an abomination in Your sight. Forgive us, O Lord; our sins are many. We repent for those who do not know to repent for themselves. Hear us, O God; answer and forgive. Send a spiritual awakening. Send those signs Joel spoke of—signs in the heavens above and in the earth beneath: blood, fire, and pillars of smoke. Let the sun be darkened and the moon turn to blood. Let the unbelievers be shocked out of their complacency. Hear, O Lord, and answer. I pray this in the name of Jesus.

I lift up our president and his cabinet. Let Your will be done in them. I pray for each member of Congress, both house and senate. May they do the things that are right in your sight. I pray for the Supreme Court. Watch over the decisions they are called upon to make. Cause them to judge righteously. I lift up the commanders of our armed forces and all of our military personnel. Let there be peace and not war, we pray. In Jesus' name.

And now, Lord, I pray: give us this day our daily bread. You are my source. Your hand, Lord, supplies my needs, and I thank You. You are the bread of life. I need You to live. Thank You, Jesus, for life through the bread You supply.

Forgive us, Lord, as we forgive others. I confess my sins to You, O Lord. Forgive, I pray. I have set my heart to forgive. I will not take offense today. I have been forgiven, and I will forgive, no matter what anyone may do to me. I choose to forgive.

Lead us, Lord, not into temptation. Keep us from being led into wrong paths, I pray. I thank You that the Holy Spirit who lives within us is leading our lives. I have been led. I am being led, and I will be led.

Deliver us from the Evil One, Lord Jesus. Keep us alert. Point out the Evil One's traps. Let us not be overcome of the Devil but rather, to overcome—to tread on the serpent, to walk in victory.

I stand with my loins girded about with the truth. I have on the breastplate of righteousness—Your righteousness, Lord, not mine. My feet are shod with the gospel of peace. I have the shield of faith, the helmet of salvation and the sword of the Spirit.

I will pray always with all prayer and supplication in the Spirit for all men. I will walk in victory through the power of the Holy Spirit, declaring that:

Thine is the kingdom.

Thine is the power.

Thine is the glory—forever—amen.

Praise the Lord!

CHAPTER FIFTEEN

How to Put Satan in a Bind

Much is being said today about binding the Devil. Books abound on spiritual warfare, knowing the Enemy, and so forth. However, I have read many of these and have not found them to be all that helpful. It seems more often than not, readers learn much more about the power of Satan than the power of the Lord Jesus. It has been my experience that every door of my life is closed to the Enemy when I recognize the power of the blood and worship my Father, the Holy Spirit, and the Lord Jesus Christ.

The story I am about to tell may sound simple, but it helped me, and I trust it will help you, particularly, now that so many are focused on the power of the Enemy. The weakest Christian can defeat the Enemy and thwart the works of the Devil. Several years ago, I learned how important it is to live in an attitude of praise. David said, *"I will praise the Lord at all times; His praise shall continually be in my mouth"* (Psalm 34:1). The Living Bible says, *"I will praise the Lord no matter what happens."* David is saying he made a "conscious decision" to praise the Lord. I knew these Scriptures, but I am not sure I fully understood them. At least, not at the time I received the following revelation.

I woke up one morning, earlier than my normal time. While lying there in a state between being fully awake and fully asleep, I heard a conversation going on at the throne of God. The Father was asking an angel, "How is it that you do not chastise Willhite?" To which the angel replied, "Well, when I chastise him he lays it on the Devil or views it as only a 'circumstance of life' and is not helped by it so I let him alone." I was wide-awake before that conversation was finished, remembering Hebrews 12:11: *"Every son the Lord receives he corrects and chastises and that it is not pleasant. However, chastisement and correction, produces the fruit of righteousness."* The lesson I was being taught was our Father loves us and shows it by correcting us. He wants mature sons like Jesus who learned obedience through the things He suffered.

With this fresh on my mind, I began to praise the Lord for everything that happened to me, whether it was good or bad. I understood all negatives can be turned to positives when I respond appropriately. Even the bad can be good. David learned to praise and give God thanks for all things. Let me add that this lesson has to be learned over and over. We tend to forget it, at least, momentarily.

It is true that God does not tempt His children with evil. But at times, He does allow Satan to trouble one of His more mature sons. So, what do we do when we believe we are under the Enemy's attack?

Here is the rest of the story. Not long after I heard this conversation in heaven, I had the same kind of experience, but this time, the conversation was between Satan and one of his demon spirits. The conversation went like this: "Why have you let up on Willhite?" Satan asked. The demon's response was: "Since his eyes were opened, when I do something to him, he starts praising the Lord, and I know you don't want him to do that, so I've had to let up on him."

I don't know if that helps you, but I know it sure helped me. I learned how to put the Devil in a bind. All I had to do was praise the Lord!

Sometime later, a lady came to me for counseling. She was concerned about some annoying sounds in her home she believed were caused by evil spirits. She asked if I would come to her home and cast them out. My reply was, "No, but I will tell you how to do it." It is better to show someone how to do something. People need to know they have the power over the Enemy. All they need is to learn how to use it. Jesus said we are to be wise as serpents and harmless as doves. We do not have to be ignorant of his devices. By the Holy Spirit we can outsmart him.

So I told this lady to go home, put on some Christian music and begin to praise the Lord. And when she hears the noise to simply say: "Thank you Devil, you have just reminded me to praise the Lord." Then begin to praise the Lord with all her heart. I told her if Satan was, in fact, responsible for the noise, he would stop it. This is how you put Satan in a bind. Learn to respond to every situation you believe he may be responsible for with praise to God.

He does not want to be the one to remind us to praise the Lord. Try it. Do exactly the opposite of what you think Satan might want you to do. If he is trying to make you sad, sing praises to the Lord. Maybe you are not in the mood. You can change your mood. Praise is not a matter of feeling; it is a matter of resolve. I will praise the Lord at all times. His praise will continually be in my mouth, not just in my heart. However, if it is in your heart, it will get into your mouth because from the abundance of the heart the mouth speaks.

If Satan is trying to make you mad, decide to be at peace. It is your decision. We choose how we will respond. Our responses can be positive or negative. We decide—no one else.

Have you got it? You can walk in victory every day. The way of praise is the way of victory.

Conclusion

I have tried, to the best of my ability, to share things that have been a great help to me. Some of these truths I have gleaned in reading what others have said. Some have gradually become convictions based on a careful study of the Word of God. Others are what I call revelations. As I have waited in my place of prayer, God has spoken in my spirit and revealed truths that have been a great help to me. It is my prayer that in these words you have found help for your prayer life. Begin where you are. You do not need more faith. Use what you have. You do not have to be more righteous. He is your righteousness. You are not intruding when you enter His presence. He has invited all His children to approach His throne with confidence. Our Father always has time for His children. He views you as a saint, not a sinner. In His sight, we are sanctified. He adopted us. He did this because He wanted to. He did not have to get permission from anyone. He is God. He has all power and authority. Determine now that your house, that house in which you live by His permission, will be a house of prayer.

Establish a place; set a time; follow the pattern Jesus gave, and become a person of prayer.

PRAYER

And now, Father, let the mantle of prayer come upon all who earnestly desire it. This I pray in the wonderful name of Jesus our Lord. Amen!

One final thought…

If you have purchased this book on Amazon and it makes a difference in your life, please consider writing a review to encourage others in their search for answers.

www.ingramcontent.com/pod-product-compliance
Lightning Source LLC
LaVergne TN
LVHW051515080426
835509LV00017B/2074